ORAL COMMUNICATION TESTING:
A Handbook for the Foreign Language Teacher

Cathy Linder, *editor*

with the collaboration of Louise Péloquin
Project of the AATF Testing Commission

National Textbook Company
a division of *NTC Publishing Group* • Lincolnwood, Illinois USA

1994 Printing

Preface

This handbook is a compendium of communication testing techniques submitted by French teachers from the United States, France, and Canada. All contributions are based on the observations of these teachers in their own classrooms, concerning their students' wants and needs, likes and dislikes, abilities and interests. It is meant to be a first step into the domain of communication testing, and, as such, is by no means "The Complete . . ." anything. We of the AATF Testing Commission aspire only to share with our colleagues what we believe to be some practical ways to integrate the evaluation of communication skills into any existing foreign-language program. We certainly welcome all comments, constructive criticism, and/or new ideas that our readers have to offer.

In order to prepare the contents of this book, the AATF Testing Commission solicited material from three sources. An announcement was placed in the January 1976 issue of the *AATF National Bulletin*, requesting that members submit tests that could be used to evaluate communication skills. In May 1976 a memo was sent to directors of summer workshops on communication, explaining the purpose of the tests that were to be included and describing the three types of communication activities. They were asked to invite their workshop participants to create communication tests. In the summer of 1976, teachers enrolled in a communication seminar given by Rebecca Valette at the Middlebury College French School were encouraged to develop appropriate materials. Finally, in August 1976, there was a sufficient amount of material to begin compiling a manuscript.

The AATF Testing Commission is one of several commissions established in 1973 by Professor Douglas Alden, president of the association at that time, to consider pragmatic issues facing French teachers. In 1975, under the co-chairmanship of Rebecca Valette and Robert Vicars, the testing commission decided to prepare a series of books dealing with topics of interest to language teachers, of which this is the first to appear in print.

The production of this book is due to the efforts of the 1975–76 members of the testing commission, who gave their time and energies to its creation: members William Bellion, Anna Harrington, Susan Kullberg, Priscille Michaud, Gary Rossi, Robert Vicars, and consultant John Riordan. In particular, I would like to thank Marie-Claude Laforest for her patient editing of all of the French to assure its naturalness; Louise Péloquin for her invaluable help with the introduction to the book; and most especially Rebecca Valette, whose hard work, persistence, and encouragement were the decisive factors behind this publication. (The members of the testing commission would welcome your comments. Please send them to Cathy Linder or Robert Vicars, c/o National Textbook Company, 8529 Niles Center Road, Skokie, Illinois 60076.)

Cathy Linder, editor
Middlebury, Vermont

Contents

Part One:
An Introduction to
Oral Communication Testing

1. What is Communication?

Language is the most developed form of communication and one of humankind's finest inventions. It not only provides a means of self-expression but also serves as a tool for describing the world from which it originated. Language is meant to be used as a means of communication of emotions, or ideas, or culture. Why, then, should so many of those who teach what we call "foreign" language insist on making every lesson an exercise in meaningless structural manipulation or dialogue memorization rather than teaching language in its practical context? Each student ought to be able to say, "This language is not only fun to learn, and not only have I found a new way of looking at the world, but this is something I can really put to practical use when I need to, and it has taught me a great deal about how my native language works as well." It is only when students come to these realizations or, at the very least, acquire a positive attitude and the desire to continue their studies, can teachers say that they have been successful.

People develop their identities and present them to others through communication. Consequently, communication helps the processes of growth and maturity of the individual. People want to understand and be understood: communication activities contribute to emotional, psychological, and social satisfaction. It is essential for us, as teachers, to present the second language as a tool of personal expression so that students will be able to use what they learn to express their thoughts and emotions freely. In this context learning a language becomes a matter of personal development rather than a study of abstractions. Studying a language must lead to practical application—use—of that language.

Before we even begin to think about teaching communication, we first must define our terminology. When we speak of "communicating" in the everyday sense of the word, we mean three things: *listening for communication*, a situation in which a person must understand the spoken language in order to obtain certain necessary information (for example, directions for getting from one place to another, the movie schedule for Saturday night, the gist of a telephone message, etc.); *oral expression*, where a person must be able to convey specific information to someone else (for example, giving someone directions, explaining how a certain appliance works, teaching someone the rules of a game, etc.); and *conversation*, which is any exchange of unrehearsed dialogue between two or more people that can include anything from an everyday exchange of greetings, to returning an unwanted item to a store, to having an argument with parents about the "rules of the house."

What has probably prevented many teachers from introducing communication activities into the classroom is the fact that there is very little resource material available. Only recently have textbooks started including exercises in communication, and even in those cases where communication exercises exist, hardly any provisions are made for testing this very important facet of learning. In the second half of this book, we have provided numerous examples of how communication can be tested. One advantage of communication tests that does not exist in any standard grammar test is the option of using the test itself as a teaching device, with very little or no necessary preparation by the students. These tests also require minimal preparation by the teacher. All in all, then, teaching communication in the foreign-language classroom becomes a meaningful activity with a dual function: learning and evaluating. More importantly, communication activities leave students with a sense of accomplishment of having acquired a useful skill.

2. What Is a Communication Test?

Communicative competence is measured according to the degree of fluency with the spoken language, but it also includes comprehension of that language in a "real-life" situation. Demands, exclamations, description, narration, explanation—these are the facets of language that should concern us. We must measure whether or not the message has been transmitted. In real life, the meaning of the message is more important than its linguistic form; therefore, it is essential to distinguish errors that inhibit the transmission of the message from those which do not. To demand grammatical exactness on a communication test is not realistic for the students: linguistic competence, in short, is not communicative competence.

The test, if it is to be a valid one, must parallel a real communication situation as closely as possible. How can such a test be graded? There are two important criteria: first, the evaluation must be based on the ability to communicate and not upon the "other" elements, such as exact pronunciation and grammatical structures; second, the results of the scoring must be sufficiently reliable. In the evaluation of a communication test, there may be a tendency to confuse the purely linguistic abilities of the student with communicative competence. The result of this mixture is the diminution of the validity of the test. It is therefore essential that the examiner base the grade solely on the student's ability to communicate well in a given situation.

The four integral elements of communication are *fluency*, *comprehensibility*, *amount of communication*, and *quality of communication*. These elements serve as the basis for a general scoring system adapted from the Foreign Service Institute (FSI) rating procedures by Walter H. Bartz and Renate A. Schulz,[1] and provide a complete and objective means of evaluating a communicative

1. Renate A. Schulz and Walter H. Bartz, "Free to Communicate," *ACTFL Review of Foreign Language Education* 7, in *Perspective: A New Freedom*, ed. Gilbert A. Jarvis (Skokie, Ill.: National Textbook Company, 1975), p. 84.

5

performance. A student receives a total score ranging between 0 and 24, depending upon the following criteria:

I. *Fluency*
   General definition: Fluency does not refer to absolute speed of delivery, since native speakers of any language often show wide variations in this area. Fluency refers to overall smoothness, continuity, and naturalness of the student's speech, as opposed to pauses for rephrasing sentences, groping for words, and so forth.
   Definition of each level on the scale:
   1. Very many unnatural pauses, very halting and fragmentary delivery.
   2. Quite a few unnatural pauses, frequently halting and fragmentary delivery.
   3. Some unnatural pauses, occasionally halting and fragmentary delivery.
   4. Hardly any unnatural pauses, fairly smooth and effortless delivery.
   5. No unnatural pauses, almost effortless and smooth, but still perceptibly nonnative.
   6. As effortless and smooth as speech of native speaker.

II. *Comprehensibility*
   General definition: Comprehensibility refers to the ability of the student to make himself understood—to convey meaning.
   Definition of each level on the scale:
   1. No comprehension—couldn't understand a thing the student said.
   2. Comprehended small bits and pieces, isolated words.
   3. Comprehended some phrases or word clusters.
   4. Comprehended short simple sentences.
   5. Comprehended most of what the student said.
   6. Comprehended all of what the student said.

III. *Amount of communication*
   General definition: Amount of communication refers to the quantity of information relevant to the communicative situation the student is able to convey.
   Definition of each level of the scale:
   1. Virtually no relevant information was conveyed by the student.
   2. Very little relevant information was conveyed by the student.
   3. Some relevant information was conveyed by the student.
   4. A fair amount of relevant information was conveyed by the student.
   5. Most relevant information was conveyed by the student.
   6. All relevant information was conveyed by the student.

IV. *Quality of communication*
   General definition: Quality of communication refers to the linguistic (grammatical) correctness of the student's statements.

Definition of each level on the scale:

1. No statements were structurally correct.
2. Very few statements were structurally correct.
3. Some statements were structurally correct, but many structural problems remain.
4. Many correct statements, but some problems remain with structures.
5. Most statements were structurally correct; only minor problems with structure.
6. All statements were structurally correct.

There is no reason why every test a student takes must be graded on a scale of 0 to 100. In fact, students may feel less pressure to compete to be "the best" when there is not a large separation between the highest and lowest grades—they will be able to relax more, enjoy what they are doing more, and, consequently, learn better. The weaker students will be encouraged to participate for this same reason, and it is perhaps they who will profit most from a situation where there is a lessened amount of anxiety. As a result, everyone comes out ahead: the students, because they gain useful knowledge at a nonthreatening price, and the teachers, because they gain the students' confidence and respect. The ambiance of the class itself improves when all members realize they can speak what is on their minds.

3. Listening Comprehension

Of all the time spent in communicative activities, adults devote 45 percent of their energies to listening, 30 percent to speaking, 16 percent to reading, and 9 percent to writing.[1] If our aim is to teach a living language to our students, it is essential that we spend time encouraging and evaluating their listening comprehension. Within the context of communication, listening comprehension pertains only to the success of the transmission of the message, not to the discrimination of certain sounds or to the identification of grammatical structures in an oral passage. These latter elements are easy enough to evaluate: examples of such tests can be found in pedagogical books (for example, in *A Practical Guide to the Teaching of French*, by Wilga Rivers, and *Modern Language Testing*, by Rebecca Valette).

The ability to understand does not only stem from what is known of the phonology and semantics of a language, however. Even for native speakers there are obstacles to comprehension because of the existence of all the possible interpretations and potential misinterpretations of words and ideas. Listening comprehension is an *active* process, and therefore one of our major goals in teaching communication should be that our students be able to seize the message in a real situation.

Several educators say that, in general, perfection of listening comprehension necessarily signifies progress in the spoken language.[2] The student must understand well in order to form the sounds well. Asher thinks that listening comprehension is so important that he advises devoting one semester on the university level or six months on the secondary level exclusively to listening skills. The listening ability must be developed to the point where the students can

1. Wilga Rivers, *A Practical Guide to the Teaching of French* (New York: Oxford University Press, 1975), p. 58.
2. M. Finocchiaro and M. Bonomo, *The Foreign Language Learner: A Guide for Teachers* (New York: The Regents Publishing Company, Inc., 1973), p. 106.

understand almost everything they hear. To exercise and evaluate listening comprehension, Asher has developed the total physical response technique. Students listen to a command in the foreign language and must immediately respond by a physical action. Their training starts with short instructions which lead to longer and more difficult ones: it is not until the students have learned to listen and understand well that they will be ready to begin speaking in the foreign language.[3] This type of exercise is valid, but if it is used in a large class, it will be necessary to find different commands on the same level of difficulty for each student.

Although the most common way of evaluating listening comprehension is the multiple choice test, there are several drawbacks in its preparation and use. For example, items consisting of short questions or isolated phrases for which students must choose the correct response are more difficult to understand than short situational paragraphs. It is important to remember that the test of listening comprehension is not merely an evaluation of the students' ability to retain vocabulary. Most of the time, that is what is demanded by short questions and isolated sentences. What we want to measure is the ability to understand a spoken message in the context of real communication. It is therefore necessary to create a situation for each listening comprehension test.

When creating multiple choice items, the teacher must eliminate all ambiguity. The correct answer must not repeat a phrase word for word from the listening text, and it should not depend on the comprehension of a word which is not a normal part of students' vocabulary. The items should not measure logical deduction: it is the global comprehension of the passage that counts.[4] Good multiple choice tests are time consuming to prepare, but their principal advantages are facility of administration and ease of scoring.

An effective means of evaluating listening comprehension is suggested by Rivers.[5] She says that the ability of students to comprehend and retain can be improved by presenting them with a summary of the main ideas in simple, active, affirmative, declarative sentences (SAAD) before reading the entire text. After hearing the text, the students must clarify what they understood in SAAD sentences. Next, the teacher asks questions about the text, and the students respond, again in SAAD sentences. We see here that it is the comprehension of the message itself which is important, not all the insignificant details. Rivers also emphasizes the importance of evaluating listening comprehension as it relates to daily language use—for example, being able to understand a play, a televised program or a radio broadcast, participating in social gatherings or discussions, etc.

3. Gilbert A. Jarvis, "Strategies of Instruction for Listening and Reading," *ACTFL Review of Foreign Language Education* 2 in *Individualization of Instruction*, ed. Dale L. Lange (Skokie, Ill.: National Textbook Company, 1972), pp. 90–91.
4. Rivers, *A Practical Guide to the Teaching of French*, pp. 88–90.
5. Ibid., pp. 79–80.

Good listening comprehension exercises make students think in the foreign language: they learn to understand without being obligated to do a mental translation.[6] Valette proposes an exercise which leads to this end and which can very easily be used as a test. Many students have difficulty understanding figures and hours. They have a tendency to separate each part of the number in order to arrive, very slowly, at total comprehension of a complex number, such as *quatre-vingt-dix-neuf*. In this exercise, students write down numbers or times of day which are read to them in rapid succession. If they have learned figures independently of their native language equivalents, they will have no trouble understanding them. Items are presented in order of increasing difficulty in order not to discourage weaker students. The situation that accompanies these figures could be a person calling the operator to ask for telephone numbers or for the exact time. Obviously, this is a vocabulary exercise, but time and numbers are used every day at the train station, at the airport, over the radio, on television, etc. When introducing time, it would be in students' cultural interest to compare the French system to the American system (14h, as opposed to 2.00P.M., for example).

In everyday communicative situations, messages cannot always be transmitted under ideal circumstances. Noise, for example, may mask what we hear, but we still manage to understand the message in our native language. A tape recording with background noise will measure listening comprehension very well. We can pretend that a person is calling a movie theater to find out the schedule for different films and that a poor-quality recording is used to give the information. The students must learn to understand what they hear and write it or present it orally. They can "call" the movie theater as often as necessary in order to find out the film schedule. Scoring is based on how many times they had to "call" in order to understand the message.

When preparing listening comprehension tests, we must try to distinguish between artificially constructed discourse and authentic messages in everyday language. If we concentrate on the communication of real-life interactions, we will eliminate much of the difficulty in comprehension and, at the same time, provide students with the "relevance" they need and so often cry out for.

Playing tape recordings of authentic conversations from the target country is a marvelous way to expose students to the spoken language, giving them the additional benefit of hearing a variety of voices. A familiarity with the voice of the teacher poses a problem for the validity of the evaluation of listening comprehension: hearing only one voice all the time does not occur in real life. If the teacher introduces a variety of voices by using diverse tape recordings, records, etc., she will be able to evaluate listening comprehension in a more realistic manner.

Foreign-language teachers often have a tendency to slow down oral language considerably to help students understand better. This produces a distortion of

6. Rebecca M. Valette, *Second Language Testing*, p. 109.

the sounds of the language. In order for teachers to evaluate how much students can truly understand, they must allow them to hear the rhythm, the intonation, the pauses, and everything that is authentic and normal about the language. If it is absolutely necessary to slow the language down, it is better to lengthen the pauses between segments of the message than to slow down the words themselves. If students still have difficulty understanding the message, the tape can be replayed, or the text can be reread: not all communication tests need to have specific time limits. As was previously mentioned, the validity of the listening comprehension test is better assured when it is administered in a calm atmosphere without tension or worry on anyone's part, for anxiety can affect the ability to understand a message clearly. We must remember that we are attempting to evaluate the ability to understand a transmitted message, not the ability to retain each detail.

4. Oral Expression

Oral expression is more than simply good pronunciation and intonation; it is, rather, the ability to make oneself understood. When the goal of language teaching is communication, the program of evaluation must measure not only the exactness of expression but also the ease and fluency of the communication. Consequently, it is necessary to distinguish between the acquisition of the elements of language (pronunciation, vocabulary, grammatical structures) and the ability to transmit a comprehensible message. When evaluating the latter, and in order to be certain that the performance of each student is measured according to the same scale, a system of scoring must be established before the test is administered.

In an oral expression test, students use all the possible elements of language that will help them transmit their message. It is very difficult to prepare a precise system of scoring because the teacher has no way of predicting students' responses.

Besides the difficulty of scoring, the time required to correct oral expression tests is a problem for the teacher who has large classes. It is not necessary to administer formal tests very often. One very short test a semester is enough on the secondary and university levels. If the teacher is well prepared, he will be able to evaluate students' ability to express themselves within a five-minute period. Informal tests can be more frequent and can take place in the language laboratory. It is essential, however, that all machinery in the lab is functioning well so that the recordings will be as clear as possible. The teacher can give visual, oral, or written supports to facilitate students' responses. A well-equipped laboratory can be a good instrument to help foreign-language students improve their oral expression.

There are several ways of evaluating oral expression. For all of them, it is important to remember that what concerns us is the *comprehensibility of the message*, not the exactness of the other elements.

Oral expression tests can be facilitated through visual or oral supports. An example of a test with oral supports is the test of "declaration and response." The teacher gives the instructions orally, either in the native or foreign language. She then says a sentence with gestures and facial expression which guide students' responses. Their choice of response, promptness, and intonation are the items that are scored. This type of informal test gives very imaginative students the opportunity to express their creativity and encourages other students to listen to the responses. Here is an example:

Teacher: Je ne peux pas venir. (sad expression)

Student: Ah! Quel dommage!

A test of this kind encourages students to think in the foreign language. They do not have time enough to translate the message word for word into their native language. This type of communication also occurs in everyday life—speakers do not always have time to participate in long discussions.

In a test of free expression, students determine what they will say and how they will say it. Although a general subject can be suggested by the teacher, there is no way to predict the content of the students' responses: this is language usage in a true communicative situation.

The taped monologue is a test of free expression in which students speak about what they see or describe a series of events as depicted, for example, in a cartoon strip. Before making the recording, students must know exactly what they have to do. An instruction sheet may accompany the instructions given orally by the teacher. This type of test is best administered in the language lab.

Recorded monologues can also be administered without visual supports. The teacher provides subjects which elicit oral responses. It is preferable to present a series of three or four short subjects instead of one very long one. By doing this, the teacher will be able to measure students' oral performances more precisely—if one subject doesn't interest them, they have the option of choosing another which will inspire them to speak well.

The nonrecorded monologue is a less formal test which introduces a degree of face-to-face communication. It is most effective when the whole class actively participates, trying to identify the subject of each monologue. For example, each student may be asked to describe a film, and the rest of the class tries to guess its title.[1]

We have already mentioned the importance of constructing a system of scoring before the administration of an oral expression test. It is most advantageous to do the evaluation or to make the corrections as soon as possible after the test and to have a marking sheet for each student. Suggestions for scoring are included with all of the types of items described in Part Two of this book.

1. Rebecca M. Valette, *Second Language Testing*, p. 170.

5. Conversation

Of the three aspects of communication, conversation is perhaps the most difficult one to evaluate. In this case, the speakers must also be the listeners. They must formulate their thoughts, listen to themselves speak, listen to the messages of others, and pay attention to their expressions because sometimes gestures are more important than the choice of words. Communication can exist in spite of incorrect grammatical structures, a bad choice of vocabulary, and a foreign accent. On the other hand, it is possible for people to manipulate grammatical structures very well, always use the correct words and expressions, and speak with a flawless accent without communicating their ideas.

Conversation is obviously the most natural way to evaluate communicative competence. There are two types of conversation tests: guided conversation and free conversation. In the test of "guided conversation," two or more students act out roles according to predetermined instructions. These instructions may be given in the native language or the second language, depending on the level and ability of the students. It is important that the teacher make the distinction between the directed dialogue, which tells the students exactly what they are to say—and which often becomes an exercise in word-for-word translation—and guided conversation, which directs the students' thoughts without also directing their choice of words. The following examples of what guided conversations may look like are suggested by Valette:

1. DOCTOR'S VISIT
   Patient: You have a sore throat.
   Doctor: You discover appendicitis and send him to the hospital.

2. ORDERING FOOD
   Client: Choose whatever you like.
   Girlfriend: You like everything your friend suggests, except the dessert.
   Waiter: You are out of one of the dishes the client orders.[1]

1. Edward David Allen and Rebecca Valette, *Modern Language Classroom Techniques* (New York: Harcourt Brace Jovanovich, Inc., 1972), p. 180.

14

In addition to these guided role-playing activities, games such as "Twenty Questions" (a student thinks of a person or object, and the class must guess what it is by asking yes or no questions), or "What's My Line?" (the class tries to guess someone's profession, real or imagined, by asking yes or no questions), can be used as guided conversation activities.

In the test of "free conversation," the students themselves determine what they will say and may even decide on the subject to be discussed. The interview is a good means of evaluating conversation. This test can be administered by the teacher or an assistant who speaks the language well. In the latter case, the teacher must "disappear" as much as possible, perhaps sitting behind the student. While the assistant is encouraging the student to speak, the teacher is free to concentrate on objectively scoring the performance.

Before administering this test, the teacher must prepare a series of questions which ask for more than yes or no answers. The choice of subjects depends on the level of the students—simple personal questions (What is your name? How old are you? etc.) for beginners, a discussion about a reading for advanced students, for example. The teacher must remember that only the students' ability to express themselves in the foreign language should be evaluated.

To conclude, let us emphasize that evaluation of communicative competence must provide an enriching experience for the students—the opportunity for them to show their increasing ability to understand and express themselves in the foreign language. The test should not be an interrogation which causes anxiety and shows the students' ignorance. Rather, it should be an opportunity for them to live what they have learned and to advance towards a more complete acquisition of the new language.

Part Two:
Sample Oral
Communication Tests

Introduction

How to Use This Section

The sample tests in this section have been prepared and submitted by French teachers throughout the United States. A few sample tests come from Canada and France.

The tests are organized by category: namely, Listening Comprehension Tests, Oral Expression Tests and Conversation Tests. Within each category, the following sequencing has been adopted:

Beginner Level
Beginner-Intermediate Level
Intermediate Level
Intermediate-Advanced Level
Advanced Level
All Levels (Beginner, Intermediate and/or Advanced)

(Note: the test levels have been tentatively formulated to facilitate classification. Some teachers may find, through experimentation, that certain tests may be more successful at other levels than those indicated. It is important to read the tests carefully before administering them because some tests require specialized vocabulary, or certain prerequisite cultural information.)

Grading a Communication Test

Many of the communication tests presented in this book are scored in a manner which may seem unfounded to some, and which will probably be questioned by most, but since no performance will be absolute on either end of the spectrum, it seems to be even more unfounded and questionable to grade them on an absolute scale. For students who are working hard to learn the rudiments of communication, a grade of 95 or 55 can be both misleading and harmful. Students need to be highly encouraged as they make their first faltering attempts at communicating, and every effort they make must be rewarded. When scoring a communication test, therefore, we have eliminated conventional number grades. Instead, we have used different methods. Students are rated either on a scale of one to three or one to five, (numerical grade), or a certain word or phrase reflecting the level of their achievement, or on an open-ended scale, starting with one and going as high as the number of activities the student successfully completes. Teachers who feel uncomfortable about entering such grades in their record books may, for their own sakes, assign numerical values to the scores on the test, but students should be given the grades that accompany the test. It is not wise to give a student who is trying but who is not as able as another student a rating of 50 compared to another student's 90. It is precisely the less able students who need ego building and encouragement the most, and a low rating can have an extremely damaging effect on a student's continued effort. Communication tests, like communication exercises, should be an enjoyable part of the learning experience. We do not want to chastise students for what they don't know. We want to show them how much they *do* know and how much more they are capable of learning.

1. Listening Comprehension Tests

TITLE: Qu'est-ce que Pierre doit faire cet après-midi? (Peter's Afternoon)
LEVEL: Beginner.
SUBMITTED BY: Jill McKeever Bowers, Brimmer & May School, Chestnut Hill, Massachusetts
TEST PREPARATION: The teacher prepares and distributes answer sheets to the students. These sheets are left face down on students' desks.
ADMINISTRATION: Students are told that their parents are going away for the weekend and that they are in charge of their younger brother, Pierre. Before the parents leave, they tell their "child" what has to be done.

The first time the instructions were given, the "children" were not paying attention (the students listen only), so the parents must repeat them a second time. After the second reading, the children understand the messages. (The students turn their sheets over and answer the questions in Part I in the first exercise.) After the third reading, they answer the questions in Part II.
SCORING: The students receive one point for each correct answer.
SAMPLE SCRIPT*

Puisque vous êtes l'aîné(e), c'est vous qui vous occuperez de la maison, pendant notre absence. Rappelez à votre jeune frère, Pierre, ce qu'il doit faire cet après-midi.

Dites-lui qu'il a rendez-vous chez le dentiste à trois heures et demie, qu'il ne doit pas oublier de se brosser les dents avant de s'y rendre, qu'il y a la moitié d'un sandwich dans le réfrigérateur qu'il peut manger, s'il a faim, qu'il y a de l'argent pour l'autobus sur la table de la cuisine et qu'il faut être de retour à cinq heures parce que votre grand'mère viendra vous rendre visite.

---

*English equivalents are given at the end of each test.

STUDENT SHEET
    I. VRAI OU FAUX? Selon les instructions de vos parents:
        1. Vous avez rendez-vous chez le dentiste.
        2. Vous oubliez souvent de vous brosser les dents.
        3. Vos parents ont laissé la moitié d'un sandwich pour Pierre dans le réfrigérateur.
        4. La monnaie sur la table de la cuisine est pour faire les achats.
        5. Pierre doit rentrer à cinq heures.
        6. Pierre et vous allez rendre visite à votre grand'mère.
        7. Vous êtes l'aîné(e).
    II. Ecoutez la question et soulignez la réponse correcte.

Teacher	*Student sheet*
1. Où va Pierre?	(a) chez sa grand'mère
	(b) dans la cuisine
	(c) chez le dentiste
2. Qu'est-ce qu'il oublie souvent?	(a) l'argent pour l'autobus
	(b) de se brosser les dents
	(c) de rentrer chez lui à l'heure
3. Pourquoi est-ce que vous dirigez la maison?	(a) parce que vous êtes l'aîné(e)
	(b) parce que votre grand'mère est malade
	(c) parce que vos parents sont fatigués

SAMPLE SCRIPT
    Since you are the oldest, you will be in charge of the house while we are gone. Speak to your younger brother, and remind him about the things he has to do this afternoon. Tell him that he has a dental appointment at 3:30, and *make sure* he brushes his teeth before he leaves. There is half a sandwich in the refrigerator that he can have if he's hungry, and there is money on the kitchen table for the bus if he needs it. Tell him to be home by 5:00, because your grandmother is coming over for a visit.

STUDENT SHEET
    I. True or false? According to your parents' instructions:
        A. You have a dental appointment.
        B. You often forget to brush your teeth.
        C. Your parents left half a sandwich in the refrigerator for your brother.
        D. The money on the table is for shopping.
        E. Peter has to be home by 5:00.
        F. Peter and you are going to visit your grandmother.
        G. You are the oldest.
    II. Listen to the questions and underline the correct answer.

Teacher	*Student sheet*
1. Where is Peter going?	(a) to your grandmother's house
	(b) to the kitchen
	(c) to the dentist
2. What does he often forget?	(a) money for the bus
	(b) to brush his teeth
	(c) to get home on time
3. Why are you in charge of the house?	(a) because you are the oldest
	(b) because your grandmother is sick
	(c) because your parents are tired

TITLE: Suivez les renseignements (Can You Follow Instructions?)

LEVEL: Beginner.

SUBMITTED BY: Renate Herpich, Sudbury Board of Education, Ontario, Canada.

TEST PREPARATION: The teacher prepares and distributes to the class a dittoed sheet with a sketch of a bedroom.

ADMINISTRATION: The teacher reads a situation to the class and then gives a series of commands. The students mark the numbers 1–10 on their sheets, corresponding to the number of the command and the location of the object.

SCORING: The students receive one point for each correct answer.

SAMPLE SCRIPT

Votre chambre est en désordre. Votre mère vous donne des instructions pour la ranger.

Ecoutez les instructions et marquez la place exacte où vous allez mettre les objets avec le numéro 1, 2, 3 jusqu'à dix, indiquant la position.

1. Mettez la corbeille à papier à côté de la table.
2. Mettez tous les livres sur la table.
3. Mettez votre affiche de Charles Aznavour au-dessus de votre lit.
4. Mettez les boîtes de Scrabble et de Monopoly sous le lit.
5. Mettez vos chaussettes dans le tiroir.

ADDITIONAL SUGGESTIONS: Instead of numbering the place where an object belongs, the students can draw that object.

SAMPLE SCRIPT

Your room is a mess, and your mother is helping you clean it up. Listen to her instructions, and mark the place where each object belongs, using the numbers 1 through 10 to indicate their proper position.

1. Put the garbage pail next to the table.
2. Put all the books on the table.
3. Put your Charles Aznavour poster on the wall over your bed.
4. Put your Scrabble and Monopoly games under the bed.
5. Put your socks in the drawer.

TITLE: Identifiez les membres de la famille (Who's Who in Your Family?)
LEVEL: Beginner.
SUBMITTED BY: Sally J. Smith, The Academy of the New Church, Girls School, Bryn Athyn, Pennsylvania.
TEST PREPARATION: The teacher prepares and distributes an imaginary family tree to the class. Below each figure is a box for that family member's name.
ADMINISTRATION: Students imagine they are going to spend the summer with Nicole's family in France. Nicole is giving them some background information. Thinking it will be easier if they have an outline of the family tree, she gives them a chart to fill in.

The teacher reads Nicole's explanation three times: the first time, the students listen; the second time, the teacher pauses between sentences so the students can fill in the names; and the third time, the students check their work.
SCORING: Each correct answer on the sheet is worth five points.
SAMPLE SCRIPT

Tu m'as demandé de te renseigner sur la famille. Ce sera plus facile, je crois, si tu écris les prénoms sur cette feuille que je te donne: c'est un arbre généalogique de ma famille. Nous en ferons une sorte de jeu, pour voir si tu comprends ce que je te dis. D'accord? Bon. Allons-y!

D'abord, nous sommes six à la maison: il y a mes parents, mon frère et deux de mes trois soeurs. Ma mère s'appelle Michèle, et mon père s'appelle Philippe. Ma soeur aînée, qui s'appelle Jeanne, est mariée, et demeure en ville. Mon beau-frère s'appelle Georges. Ils ont deux filles adorables: Marie et Marianne. Marianne est la plus jeune. Ma soeur cadette, Anne, va chez nos cousins cet été, et tu vas occuper sa chambre. Mon autre soeur, Sylvie, reste à la maison. Elle travaille comme standardiste. Etienne, mon frère, va faire son service militaire dans quelques mois, mais nous serons toujours six à la maison, parce que toi, tu feras aussi partie de la famille! Ah, oui. J'ai oublié de te dire que mon oncle Henri habite avec nous depuis la mort de sa femme.

Et voilà toute la famille!
SAMPLE SCRIPT

You asked me to tell you some things about my family. I think it will be easier if you write the names on the sheet I've given you: it's my family tree. We'll make this into a kind of game to see if you can understand what I'm saying.

There are six of us at home: my parents, my brother, and two of my three sisters. My mother's name is Michèle, and my father is Philippe. The oldest girl, Jeanne, is married and lives in the city. My brother-in-law's name is Georges. They have two adorable daughters, Marie and Marianne. Marianne is the youngest. My younger sister, Anne, will be away for the summer, and you will be staying in her room. My other sister, Sylvie,

La Famille de Nicole

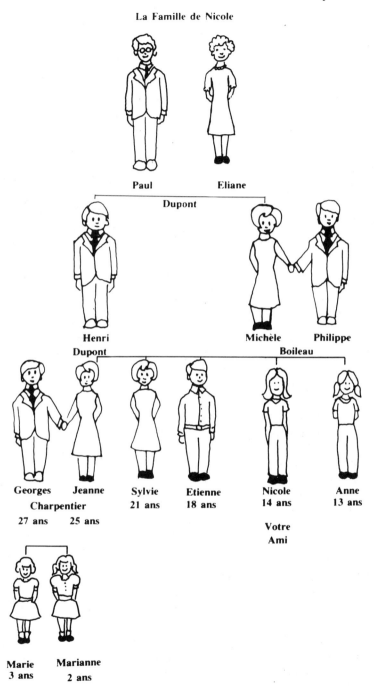

Note: Nicole's name, and the grandparents, Paul and Eliane, are filled in on the students' sheet.

will be home. She works for the telephone company. Etienne, my brother, is going into the army in a few months, but there will still be six people at home because you will be a part of our family! Oh yes—I forgot to tell you that my uncle Henri has been living with us since his wife's death.

In a few months I will have another niece or a nephew!

TITLE: **Le magasin unique et le supermarché (Specialty Shops and Super-markets)**

LEVEL: Beginner.

SUBMITTED BY: Sr. Josephine Barbiere, St. Angela Hall, Brooklyn, New York.

TEST PREPARATION: The students should be aware that the number of supermarkets is increasing in France and that many foods can now be purchased either in the supermarket or in specialty stores. The teacher has a list of ten sentences which he will either read or have recorded on tape.

ADMINISTRATION: The teacher distributes a two-column ditto sheet to each student. One column reads "SUPERMARCHÉ" and one reads "MAGASIN UNIQUE." Students are told the following: "Votre mère vous a laissé une liste de choses qu'il faut acheter pour elle. Elle a oublié de vous dire à quel magasin il faut les acheter. Elle vous téléphone."

The students listen to each phrase twice and then check the column which indicates where the mother wants the purchases made.

SCORING: Each correct answer receives one point.

SAMPLE SCRIPT

Mettez une croix sous "SUPERMARCHÉ" ou "MAGASIN UNIQUE" selon les instructions de votre mère.

1. Les pommes sont moins chères au supermarché qu'à l'épicerie.
2. Je préfère les gâteaux de M. Dupont.
3. Les petits pois sont plus frais au supermarché.
4. Le boulanger a du pain frais.
5. La salade est toujours fraîche au supermarché.
6. J'aime la viande de M. Leclerc. Achète deux biftecks.
7. Dis à M. Leclerc que je voudrais un jambon pour samedi.
8. Le café est plus frais à l'épicerie.
9. S'il n'y a pas de sucre, achètes-en à l'épicerie.
10. Si tu veux des bonbons, va à la confiserie.

ADMINISTRATION: One column reads "Supermarket" and one reads "Specialty Shop."

You promised your mother that you would take care of this week's shopping for her. She left you the list of things she needs but forgot to tell you where she wants you to buy them. She calls you from her office.

SAMPLE SCRIPT

Put an x under Supermarket or Specialty Shop according to your mother's instructions.

1. Potatoes are cheaper at the supermarket than at the grocer's.
2. I prefer Mr. Dupont's cakes.
3. Peas are fresher at the supermarket.
4. The baker has fresh bread.
5. The lettuce is always crispy at the supermarket.
6. I love Mr. Leclerc's meat. Buy me two steaks.
7. Tell Mr. Leclerc that I'd like some veal patties for Saturday.
8. The grocer's coffee is fresher.
9. If we have no sugar, buy some at the grocery store.
10. If you want any candy, go to the chocolate shop.

TITLE: L'heure officielle et l'heure courante (Two-timed)
LEVEL: Beginner.
SUBMITTED BY: Christiane Zue, Windsor High School, Windsor, Vermont.
TEST PREPARATION: The teacher has a list of ten items from a train, boat, or bus schedule. The students each receive a time "conversion" sheet.
ADMINISTRATION: The teacher reads the ten sentences to the class as they appear on the timetable, and they must convert the times from a twenty-four- to a twelve-hour clock.
SCORING: Très bien   9–10 correct answers
         Bien   7–9 correct answers
         Assez bien   5–6 correct answers
SAMPLE SCRIPT

Teacher's List	Students' List
1. le train pour Nice est à 20h.	Alors, il part à _____
2. le bateau pour Ajaccio est à 19h.	Alors, il part à _____
3. l'avion pour Paris est a 13h30.	Alors, il part à _____
4. l'autobus pour Bordeaux est a 12h.	Alors, il part à _____

SCORING: Excellent   9–10 correct anwers
         Very good   7–8 correct answers
         Good   5–6 correct answers
SAMPLE SCRIPT

Teacher's List	Students' List
1. The train for Nice is at 2000 hours.	It is leaving at _____
2. The boat for Ajaccio is at 1900 hours.	It is leaving at _____
3. The plane for Paris is at 1330 hours.	It is leaving at _____
4. The bus for Bordeaux is at 1200 hours.	It is leaving at _____

TITLE: Une invitation inopinée (An Unexpected Invitation)
LEVEL: Beginner.
SUBMITTED BY: Susan Woodsum, School District #28, Northbrook, Illinois.
TEST PREPARATION: A one-sided telephone conversation is recorded at normal conversational speed, with periodic pauses as if listening to the other party. The students are given dittoed question sheets.
ADMINISTRATION: The students are told that they will hear one side of a telephone conversation three times. The conversation will contain the answers to the questions written on the dittoed sheets.

As the students listen to the tape, they are to answer the questions in English. When the student has answered all the questions, he places the paper face down on the desk and writes the exact time on the back. Extra credit will be given for rapid completion.
SCORING: The answer sheets are corrected on a scale of 100 points. One point is added to the student's score for each minute's difference between his completion time and the end of the test.
EXAMPLE: Student A completes the test with 90% accuracy. She recorded the time of 10:14 on the test, and the last recording ended at 10:18. She therefore receives four additional points, giving a total score of 94.
SAMPLE SCRIPT

Allô, Marie? Ici Suzanne ... Il y a un pique-nique chez notre professeur de français le vendredi 12 mai vers six heures du soir ... Oui, et derrière sa maison il y a une piscine, alors, il faut apporter ton maillot ... D'accord ... elle habite une petite maison blanche à côté de la bibliothèque, au coin de la rue ... Son adresse est 295 Avenue des Fleurs. Tu viens? ... Ah, bon! à demain!

STUDENT SHEET
  1. What is going to happen?
  2. Where?
  3. What day?
  4. What date?
  5. What time?
  6. What should you bring?
  7. What color is the teacher's house?
  8. Next to what building does the teacher live?
  9. What is the teacher's address?
  10. What can you do there?

ADDITIONAL SUGGESTIONS: The teacher may prefer to give the students the list of questions the day before the test in case they choose to review vocabulary they feel they may need.
SAMPLE SCRIPT

Hello, Marie? This is Susanne ... There's going to be a picnic at our French teacher's house on Friday, May 12, at 6:00 at night .... Yes, and she has a swimming pool in her back yard, so bring your bathing suit ...

O.K. ... She lives in the small white house next to the library—on the corner. Do you know which one I'm talking about? Her address is 295 Flowers Avenue ... Will you be able to make it? ... Great! See you tomorrow!

TITLE: Omelette, aux champignons (Let's Make a Mushroom Omelette!)
LEVEL: Beginner.
SUBMITTED BY: Barbara B. Dow, Tulsa Jr. College, Tulsa, Oklahoma.
TEST PREPARATION: The instructions for making an omelette are recorded. Each student receives an answer sheet which contains a list of ingredients which may or may not be necessary for the recipe.
ADMINISTRATION: The students are taking their first cooking lesson from a friend who has an excellent recipe for an omelette. They must go to the supermarket in the afternoon to buy some things for the family, and they must decide which items on their shopping lists will be needed to prepare it. The friend calls to give them the recipe. (Note: The students will not understand the entire recipe but should be able to identify the ingredients.) The tape is played twice. The first time, it should be stopped after each sentence; the second time, it should be played without pauses.
SCORING: Students receive one point for each correct answer.
SAMPLE SCRIPT
Il faut des oeufs et du beurre très frais. Pour quatre personnes, prenez six ou sept oeufs, cassez-les dans une terrine. Salez, poivrez et battez bien avec une fourchette. Ajoutez les champignons préablement sautés au beurre, placez ensuite dans une poêle épaisse un morceau de beurre gros comme une noix, faites-le bien chauffer, puis versez dedans vos oeufs avec les champignons. Laissez prendre un moment sur le feu, puis soulevez la partie prise avec une fourchette pour faire glisser les oeufs qui ne sont pas encore pris. Le feu ne doit pas être trop vif. Lorsque l'omelette est à point, repliez-la avec une fourchette, de sorte qu'il y ait plus que la moitié de la poêle d'occupée. Laissez une minute sur le feu. Placez l'omelette sur un plat chauffé et servez immédiatement.
STUDENT SHEET

Liste d'achats	Nécéssaire?	
	oui	non
pain		
sel et poivre		
jambon		
fromage		
beurre		
mayonnaise		
lait		
oeufs		
champignons		
bacon		

SAMPLE SCRIPT

You'll need eggs and very fresh butter. For four people, take six or seven eggs, and break them into a mixing bowl. Add salt and pepper to taste, and beat well with a fork. Next, add the mushrooms, which have been previously sauteed in butter. In a frying pan, melt one tablespoon of butter, and when the pan is hot, add the egg and mushroom mixture. Let it heat up over a medium flame until the underside is slightly browned. Turn the omelette and repeat. When both sides are done, fold the omelette in half. Leave it on a low flame for one minute. Place the omelette on a prewarmed dish, and serve immediately.

Shopping list	*Necessary?*	
bread	*Yes*	*No*
salt and pepper		
ham		
cheese		
butter		
mayonnaise		
milk		
eggs		
onions		
bacon		

TITLE: Dans le Self-Service (In a Busy Restaurant)

LEVEL: Beginner.

SUBMITTED BY: Peter M. Shumaker, The Hotchkiss School, Lakeville, Connecticut.

TEST PREPARATION: Each student is given a sheet with twenty squares, each containing a drawing of some type of food or utensil, and a space to the left of each drawing (see illustration). The teacher has a list of customer orders corresponding to each of the drawings.

ADMINISTRATION: The students are workers in a busy cafeteria, and they are responsible for relaying orders from the servers to the cooks and others in the kitchen. The teacher reads them their orders, and they must mark the amount of each item ordered in the space provided in the appropriate square.

SCORING: Each correct answer receives five points.

SAMPLE SCRIPT

A. Less difficult
1. Il me faut 20 livres de beurre, s'il vous plaît.
2. Cinquante-six bouteilles de vin, tout de suite!
3. Trente-huit bols de cerises, s'il vous plaît.
4. Quatre-vingt-dix pommes de terre, tout de suite!

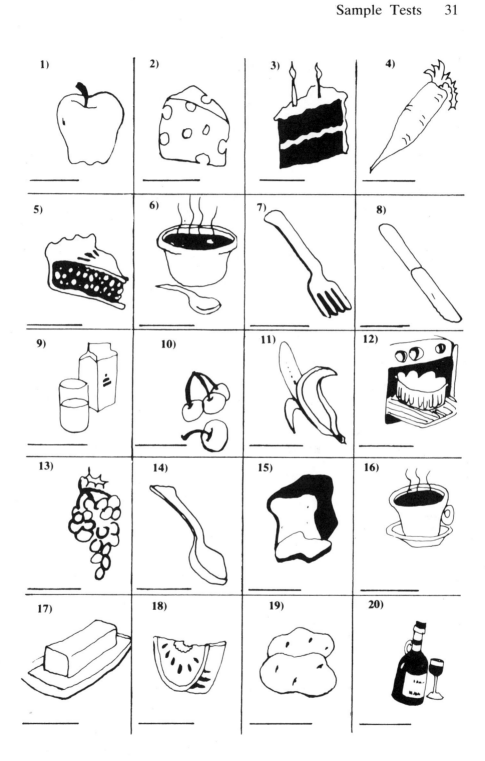

B. More difficult
1. Allez, où sont ces pommes de terre? Il nous en faut 90, sur le champ!
2. Eh, tout le monde rouspète! S'il n'y a plus de cerises, donnez-moi 70 à 80 bananes.
3. Envoie-moi 50 tranches de pastèque, en petites tranches.

ADDITIONAL SUGGESTIONS: A trial run should be given to familiarize students with the placement and meaning of the symbols illustrated on the answer sheet.

This test may be made more difficult by disguising the order, giving more information than the simple number and item desired (see script B), by giving only ten orders out of the possible twenty, or by including on the answer sheet items whose sounds are similar.

SAMPLE SCRIPT
A. Less difficult
1. We need twenty pats of butter, please.
2. Fifty-six bottles of wine, right away!
3. Thirty-eight bowls of cherries, please.
4. Ninety potatoes, and hurry!
B. More difficult
1. Come on, where are those potatoes? We need ninety, and fast!
2. Everyone is complaining. If there are no more cherries, then give me seventy or eighty bananas.
3. Get me fifty thin slices of watermelon.

TITLE: A quelle heure partez-vous? (What Time Are You Leaving?)
LEVEL: Beginner.
SUBMITTED BY: Eleanor Hooker, Cambridge High and Latin, Cambridge, Massachusetts.
TEST PREPARATION: The teacher prepares "phone calls" to a travel agency asking for train schedule information. Students are given a train schedule which will serve as the answer sheet. The teacher may tape the conversations.
ADMINISTRATION: The students imagine that they work at a travel agency. They receive phone calls from various people requesting train schedule information. As the travel agent, they must decide from the information they receive which train the caller should take. They will indicate this by placing the number of the conversation (1, 2, 3, etc.) on the blank next to the appropriate train time. The students should be given time to familiarize themselves with the train schedule. The teacher then plays the taped situations or reads the conversations aloud.
SCORING: The grade is determined by $\frac{\text{number correct}}{\text{total}}$

SAMPLE SCRIPT

I.	Agent de Voyage:	Allô, ici l'Agence Métropole.
	Client:	Je voudrais prendre un train de Paris à Marseille très tard le soir.
	Agent de Voyage:	Ne quittez pas, s'il vous plaît.
II.	Agent de Voyage:	Allô, ici l'Agence Métropole.
	Client:	Je voudrais prendre un train de Nancy à Strasbourg. Je voudrais partir de Nancy après dix-neuf heures.
	Agent de Voyage:	Ne quittez pas, s'il vous plaît.
III.	Agent de Voyage:	Allô, ici l'Agence Métropole.
	Client:	Je voudrais prendre un train express de Paris à Marseille. Je voudrais partir après 7 heures, mais avant midi.
	Agent de Voyage:	Ne quittez pas, s'il vous plaît.

STUDENT SHEET

L'HORAIRE

	Départ	Arrivée	
Paris-Marseille	4h	14h	_____
	7h (express)	15h	_____
	8h	18h	_____
	9h 30	19h 30	_____
	11h 30 (express)	19h 30	_____
	17h	3h	_____
	22h	8h	_____
Nancy-Strasbourg	7h 30	8h 10	_____
	10h 15	11h 15	_____
	14h 15	15h 15	_____
	19h	20h	_____
	21h	22h	_____

SAMPLE SCRIPT

I.	Travel agent:	Hello, Metropolitan Travel Agency.
	Client:	I would like to take a late night train from Paris to Marseille.
	Travel agent:	Hold on, please.
II.	Travel agent:	Hello, Metropolitan Travel Agency.
	Client:	I would like to take a train from Nancy to Strasbourg after 7:00 P.M.
	Travel agent:	Hold on, please.
III.	Travel agent:	Hello, Metropolitan Travel Agency.
	Client:	I would like to take an express train from Paris to Marseille. I would like to leave after 7:00 A.M. but before noon.
	Travel agent:	Hold on, please.

SCHEDULE	Leaves	Arrives
Paris-Marseille	4:00 A.M.	2:00 P.M.
	7:00 A.M. (express)	3:00 P.M.
	8:00 A.M.	6:00 P.M.
	9:30 A.M.	7:30 P.M.
	11:30 A.M. (express)	7:30 P.M.
	5:00 P.M.	3:00 A.M.
	10:00 P.M.	8:00 A.M.
Nancy-Strasbourg	7:30 A.M.	8:10 A.M.
	10:15 A.M.	11:15 A.M.
	2:15 P.M.	3:15 P.M.
	7:00 P.M.	8:00 P.M.
	9:00 P.M.	10:00 P.M.

TITLE: Numbers for Nonmathematicians

LEVEL: Beginner or intermediate.

SUBMITTED BY: John Dello Russo, Matignon High School, Cambridge, Massachusetts.

TEST PREPARATION: The teacher prepares a script of various situations in which numbers are used—age, dates, phone numbers, prices, etc. The script may be read or taped. It is essential that the speaker be as fluent as possible and not slow down for numbers.

ADMINISTRATION: The teacher plays the tape or reads the script two times. Students write each number in numerals on paper.

SCORING: Grades can be assigned by proportion: $\dfrac{\text{number correct}}{\text{total}}$

SAMPLE SCRIPT

Vous travaillez dans un petit co-op. La caisse est en panne. Le patron vous dit les prix et vous devez faire les factures pour les clients.

Le poulet coûte cinq francs.   Student answer: 5.

Vous êtes téléphoniste. Vous devez faire passer les coups de téléphone.

Mademoiselle, je voudrais soixante-seize, quarante-neuf, cinquante-quatre.   Student answer: 76-49-54.

Vous êtes fonctionnaire au Bureau des Passeports. Vous demandez aux personnes qui désirent obtenir un passeport en quelle année elles sont nées. Remplissez le formulaire avec l'information que vous recevez.

Je suis né en dix-neuf cent cinquante-deux.   Student answer: 1952.

ADDITIONAL SUGGESTIONS: It is advisable not to use expressions of time, since comprehension of this concept also requires some transformations on the part of the students (e.g.: "il est neuf heures moins le quart" gives the answer 8:45). Time can be tested in this way but as a separate test.

SAMPLE SCRIPT

You are working in a small co-op. The cash register is not working. Your boss gives you a list of the prices, and you have to write out the receipts for the customers.

Chicken costs three dollars: Student answer: 3.

You are a telephone operator. You must make calls for customers. "Operator, I would like seven sixty-four ninety-five forty-one."   Student answer: 764-9541.

You work for the Bureau of Passports, and you must find out each applicant's birthdate. Fill in the form with the information you receive. I was born in nineteen fifty-two.   Student answer: 1952.

ADDITIONAL SUGGESTIONS: It is a quarter to nine gives the answer 8:45.

TITLE: Les Coins du Monde (The Four Corners of the World)

LEVEL: Beginner or intermediate.

SUBMITTED BY: Stephen Card, The Choate School, Wallingford, Connecticut.

TEST PREPARATION: The teacher has a list of ten short paragraphs which might be written on postcards by vacationing friends. The students are given response sheets, numbered from 1 to 10. Next to each number are boxes indicating the following choices: □ de Paris □ de New York □ de Londres □ du Québec □ de la Martinique.

ADMINISTRATION: The teacher reads each postcard to the class, pausing between postcards. The student must correctly identify the origin of the postcard from the information appearing on it.

SCORING: 8–10 correct   très bien (very good)

          6–7 correct   bien (good)

          0–5 correct   essayez encore (try again)

SAMPLE SCRIPT:

Salut! Il fait un temps splendide ici! J'adore la cuisine créole et la pêche sous-marine. Demain on ira à Fort-de-France. Amitiés, Yves.

Correct response: □ de la Martinique.

TEST PREPARATION:

□ from Paris □ from New York □ from London □ from Quebec □ from Martinique.

SAMPLE SCRIPT

Hi! The sun is truly magnificent here! I *love* Creole cooking and underwater fishing. Tomorrow we're going to visit Fort-de-France. Love, Yves.

TITLE: Mon ami Microbe (Some of My Best Friends are Germs)

LEVEL: Beginner or intermediate.

SUBMITTED BY: Cathy Linder, The Windsor School, Flushing, New York.

TEST PREPARATION: Each student is given a drawing of the human body (see illustration). There will be a series of recordings, each corresponding to a different disease.

ADMINISTRATION: The students have been transformed into "germs" by an evil genie that lived in last night's vegetables. They are now under the command of the "Master Germ" and must spend their lives in relentless pursuit of healthy teenagers. Following the directions of the Master Germ, they will trace a path through the body of their next victim.

SCORING: For each disease, the germs will travel through eight parts of the body, and the students receive one point each time their path crosses one of these places.

SAMPLE SCRIPT

Voici le Maître Microbe qui parle. Aujourd'hui, il s'agit d'attaquer le corps de Marianne Gironde, pour lui donner une étrange maladie: ainsi elle va rater son examen de français: la pauvre!

Maintenant, écoutez-moi bien: la première chose à faire, c'est d'entrer par le pouce de la main droite. De là, vous suivez le bras jusqu'à ce que vous arriviez au coude, et vous tournez à gauche. Vous entrez dans l'épaule, et suivez la piste qui vous mènera à l'oreille. Si le passage est bloqué, vous devez essayer de passer coûte que coûte. Cela va lui faire mal à l'oreille, mais il y a encore des choses à faire. Continuez tout droit, et vous arriverez au centre de la tête. Tournez encore à gauche, sortez par l'oeil droit, et retournez vite au Centre Biologique pour déjeuner: il y aura un grand bol de yaourt à l'orange cet après-midi!

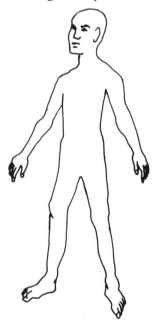

Sample sheet to accompany "Mon Ami Microbe"

SAMPLE SCRIPT

This is the Master Germ speaking. Today, you are going to attack the body of Marianne Gironde, and give her a very strange illness. She will not be able to take her French test, either. Poor thing!

Now listen carefully: the first thing you will do is enter through her right thumb. From there, follow her arm until you reach her elbow, and turn left. Go into her shoulder, and follow the route that leads to her ear. If the passage is blocked, you will have to force your way in. This will give her a terrible earache, but you still have some things to do. Continue on, and you will arrive at the center of her head. Turn left, leave through her right eye, and come back to the Biological Center for lunch: they're serving orange yogurt this afternoon!

TITLE: Système D au téléphone (How to Take Telephone Messages)
LEVEL: Beginner or intermediate.
SUBMITTED BY: Sally Sabto, Cuesta College, San Luis Obispo, California.
TEST PREPARATION: Have three taped telephone messages. Dittoed statements based on the taped passages are distributed to the students.
ADMINISTRATION: The students hear all the messages at once. Each tape is repeated twice. They may take notes to help them remember the information. After the second hearing, the students decide whether the written statements are true or false so that they will be able to give out correct information to the person for whom the message was intended.

SCORING: Très bien   9–12 correct answers
    Bien   5–8 correct answers
    Assez bien   3–4 correct answers

SAMPLE SCRIPT

Ici Mme Duclos. Voulez-vous dire à Monsieur Legrand que je ne serai pas à la réunion du cercle français ce soir parce que ma fille est malade. Demain je lui parlerai à propos de la prochaine réunion.
1. C'est Mme Dupont.
2. Elle ne va pas à la réunion.
3. Sa belle-fille est malade.
4. Elle va parler à M. Legrand plus tard.
Ici Air France. Voici les renseignements sur les vols directs à New York. Il y a un avion qui part à 11h 30 tous les jours du lundi au samedi et qui arrive à new York à 14h 15. Un autre part le dimanche à 13h 45 et arrive à New York à 16h 05.
1. Les avions s'arrêtent à Londres.
2. Les avions arrivent l'après-midi.
3. Il y a un avion chaque jour.
4. Il n'y a pas de service direct le dimanche.
Ici, Anne-Marie. Je suis terriblement enrhumée et ne peux pas aller à

l'école aujourd'hui. Veux-tu prendre note des devoirs de maths et d'histoire pour moi? Je te téléphonerai vers 6h ce soir.
1. Sa mère a un rhume.
2. Elle veut avoir les devoirs.
3. Elle nous raconte une histoire.
4. Elle va téléphoner plus tard.

ADDITIONAL SUGGESTIONS: Try the test at midyear and again at the end of the year. Compare results to judge progress.

SCORING: Excellent   9–12 correct answers
        Very Good   5–8   correct answers
        Good   3–4   correct answers

SAMPLE SCRIPT

This is Mrs. Duclos. please tell Mr. Legrand that I will not be at the French Club meeting this evening because my daughter is sick. I'll speak to him tomorrow about the next meeting.
1. Mrs. Dupont called.
2. She isn't going to the meeting.
3. Her daughter-in-law is sick.
4. She'll speak to Mr. Legrand later tonight.

    I'm calling from Air France. Here is the information you requested about direct flights to New York. We have a flight leaving at 11:30 A.M., Monday through Saturday, which arrives in New York at 2:15 P.M. The flight on Sunday leaves at 1:45 P.M. and arrives in New York at 4:05 P.M.
1. The flights have a stopover in London.
2. They arrive in the afternoon.
3. There is a flight every day.
4. There are no direct flights on Sunday.

    This is Anne Marie. I have a terrible cold, and I won't be in school today. I'd really appreciate it if you could get my math and history assignments. I'll call you back about 6:00 this evening.
1. Her mother has a cold.
2. She wants her homework assignments.
3. She is telling a story.
4. She is going to call back later.

TITLE: Pensez à la métrique (Think Metric!)
LEVEL: Intermediate.
SUBMITTED BY: Beverly DiNapoli, Fox Lane High School, Bedford, New York and Vincent DiNapoli, John Jay Junior High School, Katonah, New York.
TEST PREPARATION: The students are given a piece of paper which they number from 1 to 10 and divide into two columns which they label, "C'est possible" and "C'est bête." The teacher has a list of ten sentences, each containing a metric unit.

ADMINISTRATION: The teacher reads the sentences, and the students check the column labeled "C'est possible" if the statement is one that would make sense. If not, he checks the column labeled "C'est bête."

SCORING: A score of 7 or better would show a satisfactory control of the concepts.

SAMPLE SCRIPT

1. Je veux faire deux sandwichs. Il me faut acheter deux kilogrammes de jambon.
2. Pour nous quatre achetons un litre de lait.
3. Mon petit frère a six ans. Il ne mesure que trois mètres.
4. Le thermomètre marque 30 degrés; je vais mettre mon manteau.
5. Je veux faire une robe. Je vais acheter deux mètres d'étoffe.
6. L'auto est à 90 kilomètres de Marseille. On y arrivera en une heure.
7. Le thermomètre marque 21 degrés. Il neige.
8. Mon amie est très mince. Elle pèse 115 kilos.
9. Mon stylo mesure 12 centimètres.
10. Ma soeur a 39 degrés de fièvre. Appelle le médecin.

ADDITIONAL SUGGESTIONS: In teaching the metric system, students should not have to learn formulas and then laboriously work out math problems. Instead, they should be taught points of reference helpful for everyday life. For instance, a centimeter is about equal to a "pinkie-width" (thus 12 centimeters would be about the length of a pen—item #7), that 22° is comfortable room temperature (thus a person would not need a coat at a temperature higher than that—item #4), and that body temperature is 37° (thus 39° would be rather serious).

PREPARATION: Students label two columns "That's possible" and "That's ridiculous."

SAMPLE SCRIPT

1. I want to make two sandwiches. Buy me two kilograms of ham.
2. Let's get a liter of milk for the four of us.
3. My brother is six years old. He's only three meters tall.
4. The temperature is 30°: I'd better put on my coat.
5. I want to make a dress. I'm going to buy two meters of fabric.
6. The car is 90 kilometers from Marseille. We should be there in an hour.
7. The temperature is 21°. It's snowing.
8. My friend is really thin. She weighs 115 kilos.
9. My pen is 12 centimeters long.
10. My sister is running a 39° fever. Call the doctor.

TITLE: Des Achats pour maman (Shopping For Mom)
LEVEL: Intermediate.
SUBMITTED BY: Lizbeth Huyer, Hatboro-Horsham High School, Horsham, Pennsylvania.

TEST PREPARATION: The students have studied French shops and what can be purchased in them. They receive a sheet with pictures of a bakery, a pastry shop, a grocery, a fruit market, a vegetable market and a butcher shop.

ADMINISTRATION: It's Saturday morning, and the students are at a friend's house when they receive a telephone call from their mother. She is giving a party tonight and has forgotten to buy certain things, so she asks them to do some shopping for her on the way home. She reads a list of ten items that she needs. The students place the *number* that corresponds with the item next to the store where they must go to purchase that item. Since there are only six stores, they must buy more than one item in some stores.

SCORING: Each item has a value of ten points.

SAMPLE SCRIPT

Bonjour, chéri(e). J'ai oublié d'acheter certaines choses pour la fête de ce soir. Par conséquent, avant de rentrer, tu devras acheter pour moi:

1. six baguettes de pain
2. 20 tartes aux pommes
3. un kilo de fraises
4. trois litres de lait
5. une tranche moyenne de Gruyère
6. seize petits pains
7. dix kilos de pommes de terre
8. quatre tranches de jambon
9. trois litres de crème
10. 5 bouteilles d'eau minérale

SAMPLE SCRIPT

Hello, dear. I forgot to buy some things for tonight's party, and since I have to work late, I'd like you to pick them up for me on your way home. I need the following items:

1. six loaves of bread
2. seven apple pies
3. a kilo of strawberries
4. three liters of milk
5. a pound of Gruyère cheese
6. sixteen rolls
7. two kilos of potatoes
8. a half-kilo of ham
9. three liters of heavy cream
10. five bottles of mineral water

TITLE: La carte du jour (What's on Today's Menu?)

LEVEL: Intermediate.

SUBMITTED BY: Jacqueline Dionne Keating, General Brown High School, Dexter, New York.

TEST PREPARATION: After studying a unit on the gastronomy of France, the students will be given a prepared answer sheet with six categories. The teacher has a small paragraph followed by a list of twenty foods.

ADMINISTRATION: The teacher tells the students the following: Vous êtes chef du restaurant au Café de l'Univers à Tours. Vous êtes en train de préparer la carte du jour. Aujourd'hui vous avez au menu:

1. salade saison
2. pâté de fois gras
3. soupe à l'oignon
4. escalope de veau liégeoise
5. purée de pommes de terre
6. coquilles St. Jacques
7. glace à la vanille
8. crêpes Suzette
9. coq au vin
10. tripes à la mode Caen
11. bisque de Bretagne
12. camembert
13. fruits aux choix
14. boeuf à la mode
15. mousse au chocolat
16. bouillabaisse
17. omelette aux champignons
18. brie
19. entrecôte tartare
20. haricots verts

As the teacher calls out the foods, the students write the *number* of the food in the correct category.

SCORING: The students receive five points for each correct answer.

STUDENT SHEET:

CARTE DU JOUR

HORS-D'OEUVRE VARIÉS

OEUFS

ENTRÉES (Viande, Poisson, Crustacés)

LÉGUMES

FROMAGES

DESSERTS

ADMINISTRATION: You are the chef at the Universe Cafe in Tours. You are in the process of writing out the day's menu. Today you have the following items to offer:

1. Caesar salad
2. pâté
3. onion soup
4. veal cutlets
5. mashed potatoes
6. scallops
7. vanilla ice cream
8. crêpes Suzette
9. chicken in wine sauce
10. broiled rainbow trout
11. lobster bisque
12. camembert
13. assorted fruits
14. beef stew
15. chocolate mousse
16. bouillabaisse
17. mushroom omelette
18. brie
19. steak tartare
20. green beans

STUDENT SHEET:

TODAY'S MENU

HORS D'OEUVRE

EGGS

ENTREES (meat, fish, crustaceans)

VEGETABLES

CHEESES

DESSERTS

TITLE: Le métro (The Subway)
LEVEL: Intermediate or advanced.
SUBMITTED BY: Anne Grundstrom, University of Wisconsin, Madison, Wisconsin.
TEST PREPARATION: The teacher prepares the two scripts to be presented orally or on tape. The students will need a map of the Paris Métropolitain system for the second test.
ADMINISTRATION—TEST I: The students are told the following: Vous êtes à Paris avec vos parents, Place de la République. Vous voulez traverser la ville pour voir l'Arc de Triomphe. Vous regardez votre plan et vous voyez que l'Arc de Triomphe est assez loin. Vous décidez donc de prendre le métro et vous demandez à une Française de vous indiquer le trajet. Puisque vos parents ne comprennent pas le français, il faut traduire les renseignements pour eux. Vous leur donnerez six points de repère afin qu'ils puissent prendre le métro avec vous.
SCORING: Each correct answer receives one point.
SAMPLE SCRIPT
D'abord il faut choisir la bonne direction. Les lignes de métro à Paris portent le nom de la dernière station. Vous devez suivre la direction Neuilly. Mais il ne faut pas la suivre jusqu'à la fin—vous devez descendre à l'Etoile. Voici l'entrée du métro. Prenez l'escalier et achetez un ticket. Présentez ce ticket au contrôleur, puis continuez à pied tout droit. Dans les vieilles stations vous verrez deux portillons. Si ces portillons sont fermés, il faut attendre. S'ils sont ouverts, vous pourrez descendre sur le quai pour attendre le métro. Quand le train arrivera, dépêchez-vous, car les portes des voitures se ferment automatiquement après 30 secondes. Si vous devez changer de trains, vous pourrez descendre à une station de correspondance. Mais soyez sûr de ne pas monter vers la sortie, car si vous sortez, il faudra acheter un autre ticket.
ADMINISTRATION—TEST II: The students are told the following: En écoutant la radio le matin, vous entendez ces nouvelles: "Hier soir il y avait des innondations souterraines près de la Seine. Ces eaux sont entrées dans les tunnels de métro et par conséquent, il y avait plusieurs

accidents. En somme, six des lignes métropolitaines sont impraticables aujourd'hui.

Quand le speaker lit la liste des route inutilisables, marquez-les sur votre plan de la ville.

The teacher should present the script two or three times.

SCORING: Answers may be graded credit/no credit, or partial credit may be given for partial comprehension of the message. One point is allotted for each answer.

SAMPLE SCRIPT

1. La ligne numéro 1, Neuilly—Vincennes, est bloquée entre l'Étoile et la Bastille.
2. La ligne numéro 2, Pte Dauphine—Nation, est impassable entre Place Clichy et Stalingrad, et entre Belleville et Nation.
3. La ligne numéro 4, Pte d'Orléans—Clignancourt, est inutilisable entre Pte d'Orléans et l'Odéon.
4. La ligne numéro 6, Nation—Etoile, est fermée entre l'Etoile et la Motte Picquet.

ADMINISTRATION—TEST III: The teacher should present the following script twice:

Vous allez visiter Paris pendant le mois d'août et vous desirez des renseignements sur le métro. Pour mieux expliquer le système métropolitain en France, votre ami français fait une comparaison entre le métro de New York et celui de Paris. Afin de vous souvenir de ce qu'il dit, faites une liste des ressemblances et des différences entre les deux systèmes métropolitains, selon ce qu'il vous dit.

SCORING: The students cite seven of the nine differences. Each one is worth one point.

SAMPLE SCRIPT

A New York il y a trois sociétés de transport publique, le BMT, le IRT et le IND. Chaque société a ses propres lignes, qui se distinguent par un numéro ou par une lettre. Il n'y a pas de correspondances entre les lignes des sociétés différentes. Cependant, ces trois sociétés ont beaucoup en commun. D'abord, il faut acheter des jetons qui coûtent 50 "cents" chacun, c'est-à-dire, à peu près deux francs. En outre, il n'y a qu'une classe et il n'y a pas de places réservées aux vieillards, aux femmes enceintes ni aux handicapés. De plus, les métros roulent très vite parce que les stations sont très éloignées les unes des autres. Le métro de Paris est tout à fait différent. D'abord, il n'y a qu'une société de transport et par conséquent, il y a plusieurs stations de correspondance entre les lignes. Les directions différentes portent le nom de la dernière station dans chaque direction. Dans le métro français il y a deux classes—première et seconde—et les tickets—non pas les jetons—coûtent respectivement 30 cents et 20 cents, c'est-à-dire, 1F20 et 1F chacun. Il existe aussi des carnets de 10 tickets qui coûtent 11F et des cartes d'abonné. De plus, il y a des priorités de sièges données aux femmes enceintes, aux vieillards et aux mutilés de guerre. Enfin, les trains ne roulent pas aussi vite que ceux de New York parce qu'il y a beaucoup de stations très proches les unes des autres.

ADMINISTRATION—TEST I: You are in Paris with your parents at the Place de la République. You want to get across town to see the Arch of Triumph. Looking at your map, you see that the Arch of Triumph is pretty far from where you are. You decide to take the subway, and you ask a French girl for instructions on how to get there. Since your parents don't understand French, you have to explain her instructions to them in English. After the French girl has given you the directions, you will tell your parents six important facts that will help them get there with you.

SAMPLE SCRIPT

First of all, you must choose the right direction. The Paris subway lines are marked with the name of the last station. You must take the Neuilly line, but don't take it to the end—get off at the Etoile station. There is the subway entrance. Go downstairs and buy your ticket. Give this ticket to the ticket collector, and continue straight ahead. In the old stations, you'll see two large iron doors. If they are closed, you'll have to wait. If they are open, you can walk onto the platform to wait for the train. When the train arrives, get in quickly because the car doors close automatically after thirty seconds. If you have to change trains, you can get off at a transfer station. But be careful not to go out the exit, because if you leave, you'll have to buy another ticket.

ADMINISTRATION—TEST II: While listening to the raio this morning, you hear the following announcement:

Last night, there was underground flooding near the Seine River. The water entered the subway tunnels, and as a result of this, there were several accidents. Today, six subway lines are partially out of service.

When the speaker reads the list of the unaccessible lines, mark them on your map.

SAMPLE SCRIPT

1. Line number 1, Neuilly-Vincennes, is blocked between L'Etoile and la Bastille.
2. Line number 2, Pte-Dauphine-Nation, is impassible between Place Clichy and Stalingrad and between Belleville and Nation.
3. Line number 4, Pte d'Orleans-Clignancourt, is out of service between Pte d'Orleans and l'Odeon.
4. Line number 6, Nation-Etoile, is closed between l'Etoile and la Motte Piquet.

ADMINISTRATION—TEST III: You are going to go to Paris in August, and you need some information about the subway. In order to give you a better idea of what the Paris system is like, your French friend compares it with the New York City system. Make a list of the similarities and differences between the two subway systems so you will remember what he tells you.

SAMPLE SCRIPT

In New York, there is one public transportation system comprised of three lines: the BMT, the IRT, and the IND. Each line has its own trains, which are distinguished by a number or a letter. There are no transfers between the different lines. However, these three systems have a lot in common. First of all, you have to buy tokens which cost fifty cents apiece (approximately two francs). There is only one class, and there are no seats reserved for the elderly, pregnant women, or handicapped people. The subways travel very quickly, because the stations are very far apart.

The Paris subway is completely different. There is only one transportation system, and there are several transfer stations between the different lines. The direction of the train is indicated by a sign on which is written the name of the terminal station. In the Paris subway, there are two classes—first and second—and the tickets—not the tokens—cost one franc twenty centimes and one franc, respectively. You can also buy books of ten tickets which cost eleven francs. Some seats are reserved for pregnant women, the elderly, and handicapped people. The subways don't travel as quickly as the New York subway because the stations are fairly close together.

TITLE: Epreuve d'Exactitude (How Close Can You Get?)

LEVEL: Intermediate or advanced.

SUBMITTED BY: James P. Dalton-Thompson, Cranbrook/Kingswood Schools, Bloomfield Hills, Michigan.

TEST PREPARATION: All indicator words will have been previously presented to students in first and second-year courses.

ADMINISTRATION: The test is administered in the language lab. The teacher reads each of fifteen instructions individually and allows time for the students to mark their papers appropriately. After the last instruction is given, the teacher reads all fifteen in sequence at a moderate rate of speed. The second reading will not have pauses between each instruction.

SCORING: The notations of "excellent" (15 correct), "très bien," "very good," (14 correct), and "bien," "good" (12–13 correct) will be used. With fewer than 12 correct answers, no notation will be used.

ADDITIONAL SUGGESTIONS: It is helpful to keep a variety of five or six of these "épreuves d'exactitude" for use at the end of an hour when just a few minutes remain. The students enjoy them, and the content can be altered to concentrate more on numbers, directions, or new vocabulary words.

SAMPLE SCRIPT

Au professeur: Lisez chaque phrase une fois seulement. N'allez pas trop vite. A la fin de la quinzième phrase, relisez toutes les quinze, sans vous arrêter après chaque phrase.

1. Mettez votre nom en bas de la page à gauche.
2. Ecrivez la date de votre anniversaire sur la troisième ligne du papier.
3. Mettez les numéros impairs de 0 à 15 en haut de la page à droite.
4. Au centre de la page, dessinez un triangle sens dessus dessous.
5. Au coin gauche du triangle, mettez la première lettre de votre nom de famille.
6. Dans le triangle écrivez votre âge.
7. Sous le triangle, n'écrivez rien.
8. Au verso de cette feuille, dessinez une étoile à cinq branches.
9. Au dessus de l'étoile, mettez les numéros qui sont des multiples de 3, de 0 à 22.
10. En haut du verso, dessinez un petit bonhomme.
11. Derrière le bonhomme, dessinez une voiture.
12. Derrière le bonhomme mais devant la voiture, mettez un cercle.
13. A gauche du triangle, écrivez vos initiales.
14. Sous les initiales, écrivez le nombre de jours du mois d'août.
15. Ajoutez tous les chiffres sur cette feuille, et mettez le numéro dans une boîte au bas de la page au centre.

SAMPLE SCRIPT

To the teacher: Read each sentence once. Do not read too quickly. After the fifteenth sentence, reread all fifteen in sequence without pausing between sentences.

1. Put your name in the lower left-hand corner of the paper.
2. Write your birthdate on the third line.
3. Write the odd numbers from zero to fifteen in the top right-hand corner.
4. In the center of the paper, draw a triangle.
5. In the left corner of the triangle, write the first letter of your last name.
6. In the triangle, write your age.
7. Don't write anything underneath the triangle.
8. On the back of this paper, draw a five-pointed star.
9. Above the star, write the numbers which are multiples of three from zero to twenty-two.
10. On the top of the paper, draw a small man.
11. Behind the man, draw a car.
12. Behind the man, but in front of the car, draw a circle.
13. To the left of the triangle, write your initials.
14. Under your initials, write the number of days in the month of August.
15. Add all the numbers on your paper, and put the total in a box on the bottom of the paper in the center.

TITLE: L'émission française (A French Broadcast)
LEVEL: Intermediate or advanced.
SUBMITTED BY: Patricia A. Haupt, Palmyra Area Senior High, Palmyra, Pennsylvania.

TEST PREPARATION: The teacher prepares a French school radio broadcast. The students are given a sheet with questions referring to the broadcast.

ADMINISTRATION: The broadcast should be read twice at normal speed—perhaps as part of the morning announcements or at the beginning of the class period. The students are to be the coordinators of the broadcast and must be able to answer any questions posed by the listening audience.

SCORING: The students receive one point for each question answered correctly.

SAMPLE BROADCAST:

Mesdemoiselles, Mesdames, Messieurs, bonjour! Aujourd'hui, c'est le 15 septembre, 1976. Il est midi juste et voici l'émission française du Lycée de Palmyra.

Ici Pierre Cameron avec les informations du jour.

D'abord, les membres des "Francophones," le cercle français de notre lycée, bien entendu, viennent d'élire leur président pour cette année, Christophe Martin. Les 37 membres des "Francophones" l'ont élu à l'unanimité. Christophe fait sa quatrième année de français. J'ai eu l'occasion de l'interviewer et il est en train de faire ses projets pour l'année. Quoique le programme ne soit pas encore complètement établi, un des buts principaux du président est la présentation d'un Grand Bal de Mardi Gras. Christophe va insister que tous ceux qui y assisteront viennent déguisés comme des personnages français. Il me semble que, sous la direction de Monsieur Martin, le club français sera très actif cette année. Bravo les Francophiles! Maintenant, les SPORTS!

L'équipe de basket a gagné son dernier match contre le lycée de Hershey, 132 à 130. Comme vous le savez, l'équipe de Hershey était championne de l'état l'année dernière. Ce vendredi, dans notre gymnase, il y aura un match contre l'équipe de Harrisburg. Le Conseil des étudiants a organisé un petit bal après ce match. Venez tous nombreux!

Aujourd'hui, au déjeuner, il y aura de la soupe aux tomates, du steak-frites, et comme dessert, de la glace au chocolat. Il est maintenant midi dis. Bon appétit! A demain!

STUDENT SHEET

Répondez OUI ou NON aux questions suivantes:

1. Est-ce qu'il y a environ une quarantaine d'élèves qui font partie du cercle français?
2. Est-ce que Christophe Martin a été élu vice-président du cercle français?
3. Est-ce que la soupe du jour est la soupe aux tomates?

ADDITIONAL SUGGESTIONS: Completion statements may be substituted for the yes/no questions.

Complétez les renseignements suivants:

Martin: Christophe Martin a été élu _____ du cercle français.

Denise: Le prochain match de basket sera contre l'équipe de _____.

SAMPLE BROADCAST

Good morning, ladies and gentlemen! Today is September 15, 1976. It is exactly twelve noon, and this is the French broadcast from Palmyra High School.

This is Peter Cameron with today's news.

Firstly, the thirty-seven members of Palmyra's French Club have just unanimously elected a new president, Christophe Martin. This is Christophe's fourth year of French. I had the chance to interview him, and it seems that he is making many plans for this coming year. Although his entire program is not established yet, one of Christophe's main goals is the sponsoring of a grand ball for the Mardi Gras. Anyone who wants to attend will have to come disguised as a famous French personality. It seems to me that under Christophe's direction, the French club is going to have a very exciting and busy year.

Now for the sports report. The basketball team won its last game against Hershey High, 132 to 130. As you know, the members of the Hershey team won the state championship last year. This Friday, in our gym, there will be a game against the Harrisburg team. The student government has organized a dance after the game. Come one, come all!

Today's lunch consists of tomato soup, hamburgers and French fries, and chocolate ice cream for dessert.

It is now 12:10. Hearty appetite! See you tomorrow!

STUDENT SHEET

TRUE or FALSE

There are approximately forty students in the French club._____

Christophe Martin was elected vice-president of the French club._____

The soup of the day is tomato soup._____

Fill in the blanks with the correct information.

Christophe Martin was elected _____ of the French club.

The next basketball game will be played against the_____ team.

TITLE: Pour conduire un deux-roues en France (How to Drive a "Two-Wheeler" in France)

LEVEL: Advanced.

SUBMITTED BY: Françoise L. Bonnemoy, American School of Paris, Saint-Cloud, France.

TEST PREPARATION: A recording is made of a one-sided phone conversation to the Auto-Ecole du Carrefour. The students are given a multiple choice answer sheet. They must know that "deux-roues" refers to all types of two-wheeled vehicles with an engine.

ADMINISTRATION: The student has just bought a "cyclomoteur" in France and calls up the Auto-Ecole to find out the rules and regulations concerning its operation. The teacher plays the tape two times, and students must answer the questions on their sheets to show that they have enough information to drive their cyclomoteurs.

SCORING: Because all items are of equal importance, two points will be given for each correct answer.

SAMPLE SCRIPT

Allô, Auto-Ecole du Carrefour . . . vous avez un cyclomoteur? Alors, pour les cyclomoteurs, vous avez besoin d'une licence . . . Non, non, pas le permis de conduire; ça, c'est pour les motos! Vous avez seulement besoin du code de la route . . . Ah, vous êtes Américain? Bon, je parle plus lentement. Vous avez plus de quatorze ans? . . . Seize ans, bon, ça va. Vous connaissez le code français? . . . Non? Alors, il faut prendre des leçons de code dans une auto-école; vous pouvez en prendre chez nous; c'est quinze francs de l'heure. Ah! N'oubliez pas d'acheter un casque; c'est obligatoire pour tous les deux-roues . . . Je vous en prie, au revoir.

STUDENT SHEET

Mettez une croix dans la case correspondante:

1. Le garçon qui téléphone a
   un vélomoteur
   une moto
   un cyclomoteur

2. Il a besoin:
   d'une licence
   d'un permis de conduire
   des deux

3. Il doit passer:
   l'examen de conduite
   l'examen de code
   les deux examens

4. Pour conduire un deux-roues, il faut avoir au moins:
   dix-huit ans
   seize ans
   quatorze ans

5. Le port du casque est obligatoire pour les conducteurs:
   de moto
   de n'importe quel deux-roues
   de cyclomoteur et de vélomoteur

TEST PREPARATION: The student has just bought a moped and calls up the Central Auto School to find out the rules and regulations concerning its operation.

SAMPLE SCRIPT

Hello, Central Auto-School . . . You have a moped? For all motorbikes, you need a license . . . No, no, not a learner's permit, that's only for motorcycles. You only need to know the rules of the road . . . Oh, you're an American? OK, I'll speak more slowly. Are you over fourteen? . . .

sixteen, good, that's fine. Do you know what the rules of the road are in France? ... No? Well, you must attend an auto-school, where you can learn them. You can go to our school; the cost is fifteen francs an hour. Oh! Don't forget to buy a helmet—it's required on all two-wheeled vehicles.

STUDENT SHEET

Put an *x* next to the best answer.

1. The boy who calls the Auto-School has a
   a. motorscooter
   b. motorcycle
   c. moped
2. He needs
   a. a license
   b. a learner's permit
   c. both a license and a permit
3. He must take
   a. a driving test
   b. a rules-of-the-road test
   c. both tests
4. In order to drive a two-wheeler, you must be at least
   a. eighteen years old
   b. sixteen years old
   c. fourteen years old
5. Wearing a helmet is required for drivers of
   a. mopeds
   b. any two-wheeled vehicle
   c. motorscooters and motorbikes

TITLE: La première vue de la pièce *Huis Clos* (A Preview of *No Exit*)
LEVEL: Advanced.
SUBMITTED BY: Ann J. Sorrell, South Burlington High School, South Burlington, Vermont.
TEST PREPARATION: The students view a ten-minute videotape of the key parts of the play in which the characters and the plot are introduced.
ADMINISTRATION: The teacher gives a short-oral exam.
SCORING: Since the students have never seen or heard the play before, the purpose of this exercise is to see how much information they can deduce for themselves. The score is based on 20 points. As in France, "la moyenne," average (10 out of 20) would be considered satisfactory, and 15 out of 20 would be considered excellent.
SAMPLE SCRIPT
   A. The students must identify the main characters in the play by writing down the name of the character next to the appropriate characteristic. The list is read twice by the teacher. ·

1. Le lâche   _____ ⎤
2. La lesbienne _____ ⎬ 2 points each
3. La coquette   _____ ⎟
4. Le chasseur   _____ ⎦

B. The students must write *vrai* or *faux* to each of the following sentences, which will be read twice:
   1. Garcin est surpris par sa situation.
   2. Le Garçon est un chasseur dans un grand hôtel de luxe.
   3. Garcin affecte la bravoure pour cacher sa peur.
   4. Dans ses relations avec Estelle, Garcin révèle des caractéristiques sadiques.
   5. Inès préfère les hommes aux femmes.
   6. Inès dit: "Nous sommes entre nous," c'est-à-dire entre assassins.
   7. Estelle a tué son bébé.
   8. Estelle voudrait plaire à Inès.
   9. Inès sait pourquoi les trois sont ensemble.
   10. "L'enfer," c'est le feu, la torture dans la pièce.

Note: Numbers 1–8 are worth one point each, and 9 and 10, which require more thought, are worth 2 points each.

ADDITIONAL SUGGESTIONS: (1) It might be possible to acquire a record, a film, or a radio recording of the play. If there is no audiovisual equipment in your school, the teacher may stage the major parts of the play in front of the class with the help of other teachers or advanced students. (2) It is important to give the students a feel for the dramatic and for French as it is spoken on the stage. (3) *Aérodrame* is a prepared series (level II and III) which lends itself well to this situation.

SAMPLE SCRIPT
   A. 1. The coward
      2. The lesbian
      3. The coquette
      4. The hunter
   B. The students must write true or false to each of the following sentences, which will be read twice:
      1. Garcin is surprised by his situation.
      2. Le Garçon is a hunter in a luxury hotel.
      3. Garcin feigns bravery to hide his fear.
      4. In his relations with Estelle, Garcin reveals sadistic tendencies.
      5. Ines prefers men to women.
      6. Ines says, "We are of the same breed," and means "We are assassins."
      7. Estelle kills her baby.
      8. Estelle would like Ines to like her.
      9. Ines knows why the three of them are together.
      10. "Hell" is fire and torture in the play.

TITLE: Trouvez le voleur! (Find the Thief!)

LEVEL: Beginner, intermediate or advanced.

SUBMITTED BY: Cathy Linder, The Windsor School, Flushing, New York.

TEST PREPARATION: Each student is given five dittoed sheets with the following scenes: the interior of a house, the countryside, a classroom, a department store, the city. There will be five recorded "eyewitness" accounts corresponding to each dittoed scene.

ADMINISTRATION: The students are told that a crime has been committed somewhere, and by listening to a taped eyewitness description, they must decide, from the report, in what vicinity the crime has taken place. Because their mission is "top secret," the tape will self-destruct after no more than two hearings. For beginners, after deciding where the crime has taken place (and during the second hearing), they will be asked to submit a "crime report," including the time of day of the crime, the location of the witness, the exact place of the crime, and the nature of the crime (this may be done in English).

For the more advanced levels, the students will, after determining the location of the crime, be required to locate the witness and trace the exact path of the criminal according to the report. They must also fill out a crime report, in French, with the same details as above and locate the criminal's hideout and stolen goods.

Since the taped account will resemble a news interview, the witness will not be speaking in smooth, connected sentences as he tries to recreate the scene.

SCORING: Out of a maximum of 20 points, for beginners:

10 points for the correct location.

2¹/₂ points for each correct answer in the crime report.

For advanced students (maximum score depending on the number of elements on the tape):

5 points for the correct location.

2 points for each correct answer in the crime report.

1 point for each location correctly identified on the map.

1 point for the location of the stolen goods.

1 point for the location of the criminal's hideout.

Optional: The student(s) who have the highest score will be declared "chief," and each student after that, in order of score, will receive titles of descending seniority until "patrolman" ("officer") is reached.

SAMPLE SCRIPT

Enquêter: Est-ce que vous pouvez nous décrire ce que vous avez vu le soir du 17 octobre?

Témoin(e): Bien sûr. Il faisait nuit, et il n'y avait presque personne dans la rue. J'attendais l'autobus, mais j'étais sous un arbre et probablement le voleur ne pouvait pas me voir. Je l'ai vu

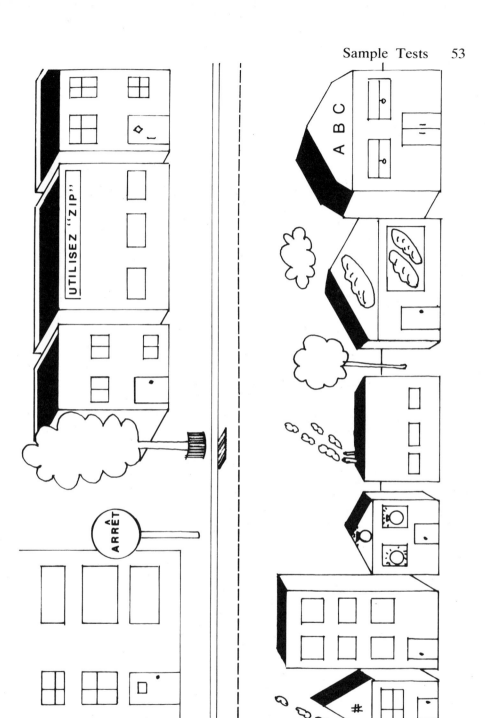

Sample sheet from "Trouvez le voleur!"

essayer de forcer la porte d'une bijouterie quand, tout à coup, il a entendu marcher quelqu'un. Il s'est vite caché dans une allée noire, près de l'immeuble à gauche de la bijouterie. Quelques secondes après, il a fait le tour de la boulangerie, puis il est retourné chez le bijoutier. Il a forcé la porte, et je l'ai vu entrer. En sortant, il avait les mains pleines de boîtes noires. Il a vite traversé la rue et est entré dans le bâtiment à droite du bureau de poste. Quand il est sorti, il n'avait plus de boîtes. Il a passé près de moi, et a disparu dans l'allée qui menait à l'immeuble blanc, en face du cimetière.

SAMPLE SCRIPT

Interviewer: Can you describe what you saw on the evening of October 17?

Witness: Certainly. It was dark, and there was hardly anyone on the street. I was waiting for a bus, but I was under a tree, and the thief probably couldn't see me. I saw him try to force open the door of a jewelry shop, when, suddenly, he heard someone walking. He quickly hid in a dark alley near the apartment house on the left. A few seconds later, he walked around the bakery, then returned to the jeweler's. He forced the door open, and I saw him go in. When he came out, he was carrying a handful of black boxes. He quickly crossed the street and went into the building to the right of the post office. When he came out, he no longer had the boxes. He passed right by me, then disappeared into the alley leading to the white building across from the cemetery.

TITLE: Mission Impossible

LEVEL: Beginner, intermediate, or advanced.

SUBMITTED BY: George Rubenfeld, University of Manitoba, Faculty of Education, Winnipeg, Canada.

TEST PREPARATION: The class is divided into groups of three students. The test is conducted outside and can be related to outdoor education courses. At a starting station, each group of students will be given directions on how to reach the next station.

ADMINISTRATION: At Station I, students activate a tape recorder or cassette recorder and listen to directions on how to go to the next station, or a French-speaking person can be at each station and give the instructions orally.

SCORING: The group that arrives at the last station first will receive 10 points. The next group receives 5 points. The group after that receives 3 points. Any other group that makes it to the last station will receive 1 point.

SAMPLE SCRIPT

Départ: Marchez 50 mètres vers le nord jusqu'à l'érable couvert de mousse. Tournez vers l'Ouest et descendez la pente jusqu'à la rivière. Vous serez à la station I.

Station I: Suivez la rivière jusqu'au pont. Vous verrez au sud une cabane à exactement 100 mètres. Allez-y. Vous serez à la station II.

Station II: Prenez le chemin sur votre gauche, comptez trois arbres le long du chemin sur votre droite sautez le barbelés. En route collectionnez des feuilles de 5 centimètres. Marchez encore 25 mètres sur ce chemin.

Station III: Tournez à gauche, marchez 20 mètres, tournez à droite, marchez 25 mètres. En route ramassez des cailloux de 10 centimètres, tournez vers le nord et marchez droit devant vous pour arriver à votre station de départ.

ADDITIONAL SUGGESTIONS: This test can be adapted to all levels by increasing or decreasing the number of stations, the length and level of difficulty of the instructions.

SAMPLE SCRIPT

Start: Walk fifty meters north, to the moss-covered maple tree. Turn west and go down the hill to the river. You will be at Station I.

Station I: Follow the river to the bridge. You will see a cabin exactly one hundred meters south of the bridge. Go there. You will be at Station II.

Station II: Take the road to your left, count three trees along the way on the right side. Jump over the barbed wire. En route, pick up leaves that measure five centimeters. Walk twenty-five meters more along this road.

Station III: Turn left, walk twenty meters; turn right, walk twenty-five meters. En route pick up stones measuring ten centimeters. Turn north. Walk straight ahead, and you will arrive at your starting station.

2. Oral Expression Tests

TITLE: Les Commentaires (Commentary)
LEVEL: Beginner.
SUBMITTED BY: John Dello Russo, Matignon High School, Cambridge, Massachusetts.
TEST PREPARATION: The teacher cuts pictures of fashion models out of newspapers or magazines and mounts them on cardboard. He prepares an evaluation sheet noting the elements of communication he desires to evaluate, such as use of vocabulary, message content, etc.
ADMINISTRATION: The students are commentators at a fashion show. They choose a series of four pictures and must say something about each item of clothing in each of the pictures.
SCORING: Using the prepared evaluation sheet, the teacher marks the elements of communication he has chosen for evaluation on a three-point scale: excellent, bien (good) and assez bien (fair).
ADDITIONAL SUGGESTIONS: The same format can be used for other topics: Le Salon de l'Auto (The Auto Show), Le Magasin de Ski (The Ski Shop), etc.

TITLE: De quoi est-ce qu'on parle? (What Are They Talking About?)
LEVEL: Beginner.
SUBMITTED BY: Martha Brassil, Lincoln Academy, Newcastle, Maine.
TEST PREPARATION: The teacher (or class) prepares a series of drawings containing elements of vocabulary that the students know. To avoid repetition, there should be one drawing per student. The drawings must be large and clear enough to be seen from a distance, and each should contain several elements about which the students can speak.
ADMINISTRATION: Four drawings at a time, labeled a, b, c, d, are shown to the class. A student draws a letter from a hat and then describes the drawing that corresponds to the letter he has chosen. The class listens, and

56

when the student has finished his description, the others guess which drawing he described. The drawing described is replaced by another, and the test continues with another student.

SCORING: This test is scored on a scale of 1–3.

1 Less than half the class knew what picture was being described.

2 About half the class was able to guess what picture was being described.

3 More than half the class knew what picture was being described.

ADDITIONAL SUGGESTIONS: This test can be used at an intermediate level for review. At a more advanced level, magazine pictures can be substituted for the more elementary drawings as the magazine pictures offer more elements for description.

TITLE: L'arbre généalogique (The Family Tree)

LEVEL: Beginner.

SUBMITTED BY: Sister Frances Hart, Bishop Conwell High School, Levittown, Pennsylvania.

TEST PREPARATION: Students are given a labeled family tree, including grandparents and cousins. There will be a tape set up in the language lab or resource center for recording the students' responses.

ADMINISTRATION: The students are parents planning a graduation party for their child. They want to invite the entire family, and they don't want to leave *anyone* out. To facilitate the task, they have made out a family tree. As they are sending out the invitations, they discuss who will be invited *in relation to their child*. Thus, they will be inviting the child's grandparents, and not their parents, the child's aunt, and not their sister, etc.

SCORING: The students are graded on the correctness of expression and on the overall clarity of the presentation. The presentations are rated *excellent, très bien* (very good), *bien* (good), and *assez bien* (satisfactory).

TITLE: Ma Famille (My Family)

LEVEL: Beginner or intermediate.

SUBMITTED BY: Phyllis S. Schlanger, Abington H.S., North Campus, Abington, Pennsylvania.

TEST PREPARATION: The teacher must find out a little about the backgrounds of the students before giving the test to avoid asking embarrassing questions.

ADMINISTRATION: The students are called to the teacher's desk one at a time while the others work on an assignment at their desks. The teacher asks a series of questions concerning the student's family.

SCORING: Depending on the clarity and creativity of their answers, the students receive grades of "très bien" ("very good"), "bien" ("good"), and "assez bien" ("fair").

ADDITIONAL SUGGESTIONS: The same format can be used to question the students about their hobbies and daily activities.

TITLE: Expliquez-moi ... (Please Explain ...)
LEVEL: Beginner or intermediate.
SUBMITTED BY: Sally Sabto, Cuesta College, San Luis Obispo, California.
TEST PREPARATION: The teacher and the students make up a list of twenty-five to thirty activities which require a description. (Examples: Comment faire un coup de téléphone, comment mettre la cuisine en ordre, comment faire du ski, comment faire des oeufs brouillés, etc.)
ADMINISTRATION: After practicing in small groups, the students draw a slip of paper from the list. In two to three sentences they describe the activity written on the sheet to the rest of the class.
SCORING: Use "très bien" ("very good"), "bien" ("good"), and "assez bien" ("fair"). Have students help by indicating whether they understood *all, most,* or *only part of* the explanation.
ADDITIONAL SUGGESTIONS: This test can be given more than once: the first time, gestures may be allowed; the second time, only words are permitted.
TEST PREPARATION: Examples: how to make a telephone call, how to clean up the kitchen, how to ski, how to make scrambled eggs, etc.

TITLE: Qui est-ce? (Guess Who?)
LEVEL: Beginner or intermediate.
SUBMITTED BY: Peter M. Shumaker, The Hotchkiss School, Lakeville, Connecticut.
TEST PREPARATION: Each student writes the name of a well-known person (TV and movie stars, people who work at the school, political and governmental leaders, etc.) on an index card.
ADMINISTRATION: Each student draws a card and describes that person to the rest of the class without giving any insulting or obvious information (example: names of films or TV shows, courses taught, governmental positions). The student is limited to a two-minute description, after which the others in the class write, on a sheet of paper, the name of the person they believe was described.
SCORING: The students are graded either $\checkmark +$, $\checkmark$, or $\checkmark -$. The teacher may score by combining two methods:
a) by her personal assessment of the quality of the description, given the relative difficulty of the selection.
b) by the number of students who guessed correctly. This second method has the drawback of relying on students' prior knowledge of the person described, although careful editing of the names submitted should compensate for this drawback. A scoring combining methods *a* and *b* should further compensate for this drawback.

ADDITIONAL SUGGESTIONS: A trial run is suggested a few days ahead of time to familiarize students with this type of test.

TITLE: Ma vie: passée, présente et future (My Life: Past, Present, Future)
LEVEL: Beginner or intermediate.
SUBMITTED BY: Sally J. Smith, The Academy of the New Church, Girls School, Bryn Athyn, Pennsylvania.
TEST PREPARATION: The teacher makes up cards to give to the students. Each card contains a different subject, such as *Ma journée typique, mon passe-temps favori, un endroit que j'aime beaucoup*, etc.
ADMINISTRATION: The student selects two cards and must speak on one of the topics. She is given three minutes to prepare her ideas and then must speak for two minutes, either in front of the class or in the language lab.
SCORING: The teacher grades each sentence individually on the following scale:
0   incomprehensible.
3   comprehensible, with major errors in vocabulary or structure.
5   comprehensible, with minor errors in vocabulary or structure.
The numbers are added together and averaged. Students receive a letter grade:
0–1   C
2–3   B
4–5   A
TEST PREPARATION: Each card contains a different subject, such as *A typical day, My favorite pastime, A special place*, etc.

TITLE: Termes des "teenagers" (Teenage Terminology)
LEVEL: Beginner.
SUBMITTED BY: Sr. Josephine Barbiere, St. Angela Hall Academy, Brooklyn, New York.
TEST PREPARATION: A list of terms used by teenagers in everyday life is prepared.
ADMINISTRATION: Students take the teacher's role and must try to explain some unfamiliar terminology to a French-speaking person. One at a time, they are told the following: A l'école il y a un étudiant français. Il passe le week-end chez vous. Expliquez-lui les termes suivants, parce qu'il ne les connaît pas:
sundae
hero sandwich
root beer float
loafers
tank top
SCORING: The students receive the grade "très bien" ("very good") or "bien" ("good"), depending on how well they have expressed themselves.

ADMINISTRATION: There is a French student at your school who will be spending the weekend with you. Explain the following terms to him, since he doesn't know what they mean:

TITLE: Comment obtenir le permis de conduire (How to Obtain a Driver's License)

LEVEL: Intermediate.

SUBMITTED BY: Christiane Zue, Windsor High School, Windsor, Vermont.

TEST PREPARATION: It is recommended that the students have recently obtained or are expecting their driver's licenses.

ADMINISTRATION: This test should be administered individually in a separate corner of the classroom or in the language lab. The teacher plays the role of the friend who is interested in obtaining his license. The friend wants to know, "Que dois-je faire ici pour avoir un permis de conduire?" The students respond with as much information as they can.

SCORING:

Très bien (Very good)   teacher understood most of what was said.

Bien (Good)   teacher understood some of what was said.

Assez bien (Fair)   teacher hardly understood any of what was said.

ADDITIONAL SUGGESTIONS: The teacher can ask questions answered in the drivers' manual or asked on the permit test, such as "Que faut-il faire devant un panneau sur lequel est écrit "Yield"?"

ADMINISTRATION: A friend wants to know, "What must I do to get my driver's license?"

ADDITIONAL SUGGESTIONS: "What should you do at a "Yield" sign?"

TITLE: Comment donner à manger au "chien de la famille" (How to Feed the Dog)

LEVEL: Intermediate.

SUBMITTED BY: Barbara B. Dow, Tulsa Junior College, Tulsa, Oklahoma.

TEST PREPARATION: Each student receives a card or a piece of paper on which is written the name of an everyday task performed in an American home. The class numbers a sheet of paper, each number corresponding to a student in the class.

ADMINISTRATION: Students play the role of parents who are going out for the evening and must tell the babysitter how to perform certain jobs. They use the format, "Pour faire ce que je t'ai demandé, . . ." ("In order to do what I've asked . . ."). After each presentation, the students write the name of the task being described on their sheets next to the number that represents the student who is speaking.

SCORING: The grade of "très bien" ("very good") is given when all or almost all of the class has guessed the name of the task. About 70% correct would receive "bien" ("good"), and 50% or below receives "convenable" ("satisfactory").

ADDITIONAL SUGGESTIONS: Tasks should be relatively uncomplicated and familiar, such as taking out the garbage, doing the dishes, making the bed, etc. The only rule is that no English trade names (such as Tide) may be used.

TITLE: J'ai oublié le mot (I Forgot the Word)
LEVEL: Intermediate.
SUBMITTED BY: Stephen Card, The Choate School, Wallingford, Connecticut.
Beverly DiNapoli, Fox Land High School, Bedford, New York.
Vincent DiNapoli, John Jay Junior High School, Katonah, New York.

TEST PREPARATION: The teacher prepares twenty-five index cards on which he draws or pastes pictures of items that one might purchase in a large department store.

ADMINISTRATION: The students are American customers in a store in France, and they are in absolute need of a particular item. The item they must buy will be decided when they shuffle the index cards and pick one from the pack. Unfortunately, they have momentarily forgotten the name of the item and must describe it to a "clerk" (a student who has been chosen by the teacher). The description may not be longer than five sentences. The "customer," once finished with his discussion, replaces the card somewhere in the deck, and the clerk must sort through the stack of cards to find the picture of the item the customer was asking for.

SCORING:

très bien (very good)	The clerk finds the product on the first try.
bien (good)	The clerk finds the product on the second try.
essayez encore (try again)	The clerk finds the product on three or more tries.

ADDITIONAL SUGGESTIONS: This test can serve as a listening exercise for the other members of the class. The teacher can ask them to raise their hands if they can give the French name for the item in question.

TITLE: Êtes-vous débrouillard? (Can You Get Out of This One?)
LEVEL: Intermediate.
SUBMITTED BY: Jill McKeever Bowers, Brimmer and May School, Chestnut Hill, Massachusetts.
TEST PREPARATION: A series of index cards is prepared, each containing a situation which is likely to occur in everyday life and can lead to serious problems if not handled well.

ADMINISTRATION: The student draws a card, reads the situation to the class, and must try to remedy the situation.

SCORING: The other students judge the solution to the problem. If they feel it will help the situation, the student receives the grade "sauvé" ("You're saved!"). If they feel there will still be a problem, the student receives the grade "attention!" ("Watch out!").

SAMPLE SCRIPT
1. Vous êtes au restaurant. Au moment de payer, vous vous apercevez que vous avez oublié votre portefeuille. Que faites-vous?
2. Vous rentrez chez vous. Ça sent le gaz. Que faites-vous?
3. Vous êtes à (Boston). Vous perdez votre chemin. Que faites-vous?
4. C'est l'heure du dîner. Des amis arrivent chez vous sans vous prévenir. Vous n'avez rien à leur offrir. Que faites-vous?
5. Vous vous heurtez à Robert Redford dans la rue. Que faites-vous?

SAMPLE SCRIPT
1. You're in a restaurant. After you get the cheque, you discover you don't have your wallet. What do you do?
2. You come home, and your apartment smells of gas. What do you do?
3. You're in (Boston). You lose your way. What do you do?
4. It's dinnertime. Some friends drop in without warning. You have nothing to offer them. What do you do?
5. You bump into Robert Redford in the street. What do you do?

TITLE: Je fais un voyage (I'm Taking a Trip)
LEVEL: Intermediate or advanced.
SUBMITTED BY: Eleanor Hooker, Cambridge High & Latin, Cambridge, Massachusetts.
TEST PREPARATION: None.
ADMINISTRATION: The students are divided into groups of four or five. Each one is given a piece of paper. Each group is going on a trip to a certain country, and each student may bring something she must describe to the others without naming. The monologue should include a description of the object and the student's reasons for bringing it. Each student begins by saying, "Je fais un voyage en (à) _____ . . ." ("I'm taking a trip to . . ."). The others guess the object and write it on the paper. Each student in the group has a turn describing an object.
SCORING: The grades of "bien compris" ("very well understood"), "compris" ("comprehensible"), and "pas très clair" ("not very clear") are given, based on the clarity of the description and the number of students who guessed correctly.

TITLE: La peinture française (French Painters)
LEVEL: Intermediate or advanced.
SUBMITTED BY: James P. Dalton-Thompson, Cranbrook/Kingswood Schools, Bloomfield Hills, Michigan.

TEST PREPARATION: The teacher has some relatively large, high-quality, color reproductions of works of art, such as *La Liberté guidant le peuple* (Delacroix), *Le fou assassin* (Gericault), *Guernica* (Picasso), etc. In addition, the teacher of advanced students may wish to introduce basic artistic terminology.

ADMINISTRATION: The class is divided into halves or thirds. The sections of the class that are not taking the test may either go to the language laboratory or work on an in-class exercise.

Each student selects a painting that appeals to him and describes it in five sentences. Their descriptions may deal with the theme of the picture, the colors, what the characters are wearing, or his personal reaction to the painting.

SCORING: The students receive grades of A, B or C, depending on the quality and clarity of their discourse.

ADDITIONAL SUGGESTIONS: After all of the students have spoken, the teacher may divide the class into groups according to the picture discussed. The teacher gives the groups half of the period to discuss the work of art. The groups then must give to the class a five- to ten-minute dissertation about their painting. The other students have the opportunity to question the group members.

Even first-year students can begin to look critically at works of art and use basic vocabulary (colors, parts of the body) to make appropriate comments. Advanced students may make use of this procedure as part of a French humanities program, where they learn to identify painters, periods, and genre, or as a basis for more sophisticated conversation.

TITLE: Un incident comique (A Funny Thing Happened . . .)

LEVEL: Intermediate or advanced.

SUBMITTED BY: Françoise L. Bonnemoy, American School of Paris, Saint-Cloud, France.

TEST PREPARATION: Index cards are prepared by either the teacher or the students. Each card contains an introductory sentence to a possible story, such as, "Vous ne devinerez jamais ce qui m'est arrivé hier: je sortais du cinéma . . .."

ADMINISTRATION: The students select two or three cards and must continue the story which appears on one of them. They are given a few minutes to prepare themselves, but written notes are not allowed. The rest of the class sits in a circle.

SCORING: Grades of "très bien" ("very good"), "bien" ("good"), and "assez bien" ("satisfactory") are given, based on imagination, humor, and continuity of events.

TEST PREPARATION: Each card contains an introductory sentence to a possible story, such as, "You'll never guess what happened to me yesterday: I was walking out of the movie theater when . . .."

TITLE: Montrez et racontez (Show and Tell)
LEVEL: Advanced.
SUBMITTED BY: Ann J. Sorrell, South Burlington H.S., South Burlington, Vermont.
TEST PREPARATION: The students bring something to class which is
related to twentieth-century France. If they are having difficulty finding
such information, the teacher can give them a list of ideas, such as
pictures, records, songs, newspapers, souvenirs, etc.
ADMINISTRATION: The students tell the class about their findings in a
three-minute talk without using a prepared script.
SCORING: Each student is given two grades (A, B or C), one for originality
and one for effectiveness of the presentation.
ADDITIONAL SUGGESTIONS: At the end of the talks, the class can
discuss the findings and ask questions about anything they didn't understand. The teacher should guide them in making a resumé of each concept
presented to the class.

TITLE: Qu'est-ce que vous feriez à sa place? (What Would You Do?)
LEVEL: Advanced.
SUBMITTED BY: George Rubenfeld, Faculty of Education, University of
Manitoba, Winnipeg, Canada.
TEST PREPARATION: The teacher prepares ten pictures representing
situations, such as shoplifting, car accidents, drug trafficking.
ADMINISTRATION: Each student comes to the teacher's desk and selects
a picture. The student must describe the picture and then say what he
would do if he were the person involved.
SCORING: If the student correctly described the picture and said in a
logical fashion what he would do, he receives the grade "très bien" ("very
good"). If he cannot describe the situation but tells what he would do in
the situation, he receives the grade "bien" ("good").

TITLE: Les Défenses (Defense)
LEVEL: Beginner, intermediate, or advanced.
SUBMITTED BY: Anne Grundstrom, University of Wisconsin, Madison,
Wisconsin.
TEST PREPARATION: The teacher and/or the students write a crime or
an accusation on index cards.
ADMINISTRATION: The students select a card which tells them the crime
they have allegedly committed. They read the accusation aloud: "On dit que
j'ai ..." and then defend themselves, stating why they could not possibly
have committed such an action or why they deserve to be acquitted.
SCORING: Following the defense, the other students indicate whether or
not the defense was convincing. They should take into consideration such
factors as delivery, logic, and content. To these global evaluations should

be added the teacher's grade of comprehensibility and appropriateness of the presentation. Students receive grades of "coupable" and "pas coupable."

SAMPLE SCRIPTS

1. Vous avez volé à la tire dans un grand magasin.
2. Vous êtes exhibitionniste.
3. Vous avez dépassé les limites de vitesse pour la cinquième fois. On va retirer votre permis de conduire.
4. Vous vous êtes introduit chez votre voisin par effraction hier soir.
5. Vous avez enlevé de l'argent de la quête pendant la messe.

ADMINISTRATION: The student reads the accusation aloud: "They say that I . . ." and then defends herself.

SAMPLE SCRIPTS

1. You robbed a department store at gunpoint.
2. You are an exhibitionist.
3. You were caught speeding for the fifth time. They are going to revoke your license permanently.
4. You broke into your neighbor's house last night.
5. You took money from the collection plate during Mass.

TITLE: Connaître les animaux (Know Your Animals)

LEVEL: Beginner, intermediate, or advanced.

SUBMITTED BY: Cathy Linder, The Windsor School, Flushing, New York.

TEST PREPARATION: Because this is a researched project, students should have access to books and/or magazines pertaining to their subject. For the demonstration, they may need any or all of the following: photographs, blackboard, overhead projector, diagrams.

ADMINISTRATION: The teacher designates a student as "camp counselor" who has decided to take the class (his "campers") on a nature hike in the woods. The counselor wants to teach them how to identify animal tracks and (for more advanced levels) how to tell how recently they were made. The counselor may use any or all materials at his disposal. His lesson should last about five minutes, and he should try to teach anywhere from three to five different footprints.

SCORING: The counselor will be judged on his ability to teach the campers. If, after seeing different photographs (or diagrams) of the same animal tracks, the campers can identify five out of five (three out of three) of the tracks, the counselor will have senior counselor status. If the campers identify three or four out of five (two out of three), the counselor will be designated junior counselor, and if they get one or two out of five (one out of three) correct, he will be a counselor in training. In identifying the tracks, the students may either call out the answers orally, identify the animal by the photograph, or both.

3. Conversation Tests

TITLE: Comment ne pas mourir de faim en France (How Not to Starve in France)

LEVEL: Beginner.

SUBMITTED BY: Michael Oates, Northern Iowa University, Cedar Falls, Iowa.

TEST PREPARATION: Each student is given two 3 × 5 index cards. On each card, the student writes a sentence which could initiate a conversation. (Example: Tu as faim?)

ADMINISTRATION: The teacher shuffles the pile of cards. One at a time, the students come to the teacher's desk, draw a card, and read the sentence aloud. An ad-lib conversation with the teacher follows.

SCORING: The grades of "très bien" ("very good"), "bien" ("good"), and "merci" ("thank you") are used. The purpose is to reward those who have communicated well without punishing too much those who are "starving." "Merci" ("Thank you") should not be a sarcastic euphemism for "mal" ("bad").

ADDITIONAL SUGGESTIONS: It is a good idea to have the students prepare the index cards a day or two in advance and to allow for a trial run before the actual test is given.

If some other person (upper-level student, amity aide, graduate assistant, etc.) is available, have her sit on the other side of the room. While the teacher is carrying on the ad-lib testing with individuals, the rest of the students are asked to prepare, in groups of two or three, one skit which they will demonstrate for the other person when they are ready. This person can grade them on the same scale suggested above.

TITLE: Chef d'oeuvre (My Masterpiece)

LEVEL: Beginner.

SUBMITTED BY: Sr. Josephine Barbiere, St. Angela Hall, Brooklyn, New York.

TEST PREPARATION: The students have acquired skills in asking questions and following directions. Each student draws something on a piece of paper (a house, a landscape, etc.), and leaves the paper face down.

ADMINISTRATION: Individually, the students describe their picture step by step so that the other students can draw it. The students who are listening may ask questions for clarification. (Example: "Est-ce que le chat est grand?")

SCORING: The grades of "très artistique" ("very artistic") or "artistique" ("artistic") reflect how well the directions were given and are determined by the number of students who have correctly drawn the picture.

ADDITIONAL SUGGESTIONS: Conversations should take place because the students ask questions to clarify directions. The conversations may lead to a discussion of the results at the end.

TITLE: Réflexions (Reflections)

LEVEL: Beginner or intermediate.

SUBMITTED BY: Sally Sabto, Cuesta College, San Luis Obispo, California.

TEST PREPARATION: The teacher makes up cards with a general question or topic on each. Some examples are: Décrivez une journée idéale. Comment sera votre vie dans dix ans? (Describe an ideal day. What will your life be like in 10 years?).

ADMINISTRATION: Students in groups of three select a card and discuss the topic in front of the class. They establish and compare their ideas and feelings and probe each other for clarification.

SCORING: Students who participate actively, who initiate conversations, receive the grade "très bien" ("excellent"). Students who participate by answering questions, or responding to other remarks, receive the grade "bien" ("very good"). Any student who participates occasionally receives the grade "assez bien" ("good").

TITLE: Au magasin (Shopping Spree)

LEVEL: Intermediate.

SUBMITTED BY: Lizbeth Huyer, Hatboro-Horsham High School, Horsham, Pennsylvania.

TEST PREPARATION: The class has studied French shops and what can be purchased in them. The teacher prepares index cards with the names of shops.

ADMINISTRATION: The students are tested in groups of two. Each couple picks a card. One student is the "clerk" and the other is the "shopper." They must engage in a short, informal conversation, including an exchange of greetings, an exchange of information about the items to be purchased including what, how many, the price, and a closing exchange including the transfer of money and products.

SCORING: The grades of "très bien" ("very good"), "bien" ("good"), and "merci" ("thank you") may be used.

ADDITIONAL SUGGESTIONS: Students may practice a similar activity two or three days before the day of the test.

TITLE: Si tu pouvais ... (If You Could ...)
LEVEL: Intermediate.
SUBMITTED BY: Sister Frances Hart, Bishop Conwell High School, Levittown, Pennsylvania.
TEST PREPARATION: The class has studied the imperfect and conditional tenses. The teacher prepares two stacks of cards: Round 1 cards contain *interview questions*. (Example: Si tu pouvais manger tout ce que tu voulais pour le déjeuner, que mangerais-tu?). Round 2 cards are *incomplete phrases*. (Example: Si j'étais le professeur de cette classe,...).
ADMINISTRATION: The students are tested in groups of three. Each student picks an interview card and a phrase card.

Round 1: One student asks the question written on his card, and everyone in the group must respond. The others are encouraged to react to the response. When all three students have asked their questions, the group proceeds to Round 2.

Round 2: Each student may take a minute or two to reflect before speaking. As each student responds to the phrase, the rest of the group is encouraged to react by agreeing, disputing, or questioning. The round continues until each person has given her thoughts on each of the phrases.

Round 3: The students relate something that they learned about one of the members of their group from rounds 1 and 2. The statements: Je me rends compte de/que: ... (I realize that ...) J'ai remarqué que ... (I noticed that ...) J'ai appris que ... (I learned that ...) serve as a basis for the conversation.
SCORING: The teacher evaluates the *participation* and the *quality of the conversation*. The student who initiates conversations, and who speaks with great clarity receives the grade "supérieur" ("superior"). A student who initiates conversations but does not speak clearly or speaks clearly but does not initiate conversations receives the grade "très bien" ("very good"). A student who makes an effort at communication without initiating conversation and without clearly communicating his thoughts receives a grade of "bien" ("good").

TITLE: Faisons un voyage (Let's Take a Trip)
LEVEL: Intermediate.
SUBMITTED BY: Phyllis S. Schlanger, Abington High School, North Campus, Abington, Pennsylvania.
TEST PREPARATION: This test follows a culture unit.
ADMINISTRATION: The students are divided into groups of three or four and are given the following outline of a projected trip:

1. les préparations (preparations)
2. les moyens de transport (means of transportation)
3. l'arrivée; les premières impressions (arrival; first impressions)
4. les gens (the people)
5. une famille (a family)
6. l'école (school)
7. le tourisme (tourism)
8. l'art (art)

The students choose the place they are going to visit and discuss at least two of the items on their outlines.

SCORING: The evaluation is based on the accuracy of the information presented and creativity. Students with accurate information and unique ideas and/or presentations receive the grade "Allez-y!" ("Let's go!"). Students with accurate information or unique ideas receive the grade, "Achetez votre billet!" ("Get your ticket!"). And students who have made an honest effort at communication receive the grade "Faites les valises!" ("Pack your suitcases!").

TITLE: Petites saynètes (Little Skits)
LEVEL: Intermediate.
SUBMITTED BY: Beverly DiNapoli, Fox Lane High School, Bedford, New York and Vincent DiNapoli, John Jay Junior High School, Katonah, New York.
TEST PREPARATION: The teacher prepares a series of cards with structured situations requiring two persons and four lines of dialogue.
ADMINISTRATION: The students are tested in groups of two. Each pair chooses one of the situation cards, each student chooses a role, and the group presents its skit to the class.
SCORING: Students who communicate well, with few errors, receive the grade "très bien" ("very good"). Students who make themselves understood with noticeable errors receive the grade "bien" ("good"). Any student who makes an attempt at communication receives the grade "passable" ("satisfactory").
SAMPLE SCRIPT

Au bureau de voyages

Client:	Demandez des informations sur les heures de départ des trains pour Marseille.
Employé:	Donnez deux possibilités.
Client:	Décidez et donnez votre raison.
Employé:	Vendez-lui un billet.

A la douane

Douanier:	Demandez au voyageur pourquoi il fait un voyage à votre pays.
Voyageur:	Expliquez-lui pourquoi.

Douanier: Demandez-lui s'il/elle a un certain article dans ses valises.
Voyageur: Dites-lui si vous l'avez ou non.

SAMPLE SCRIPT

At the Travel Agency

Client: Ask for information about the train departures from Marseille.
Employee: Give two departure times.
Client: Decide on one and give your reason for the decision.
Employee: Sell him a ticket.

At Customs

Customs Officer: Ask the traveler why he's visiting your country.
Traveler: Tell him why.
Customs Officer: Ask him if he has a certain item in his valise.
Traveler: Tell him if you do or not.

TITLE: Le Soap-Opera Français (A French Soap-Opera)
LEVEL: Intermediate.
SUBMITTED BY: Sister Mary Alisa Lyons S.N.D., Notre Dame Academy, Chardon, Ohio.
TEST PREPARATION: The students are divided into groups of two to six to prepare supplementary dialogues from the text. An alternative would be to have the students create original dialogues. It is recommended that they make use of appropriate costumes, props, gestures, etc., which would enhance the skit.
ADMINISTRATION: The students work in groups during two class periods, rehearsing their dialogues, while the teacher circulates, giving advice, suggestions, etc.

Videotape equipment is set up the period before the class. Each group presents its five-minute dialogue, which is recorded on videotape.
SCORING: The following day, the videotape is replayed. Each student evaluates everyone in the class, including himself, according to the following criteria: pronunciation, expression, gestures, intonation, rhythm. The following scale may be used:
5   supérieur (superior)
4   très bien (very good)
3   bien (good)
2   passable (satisfactory)
1   faible (fair)

TITLE: Au syndicat d'initiative (At the Visitor's Center)
LEVEL: Intermediate.
SUBMITTED BY: Peter M. Shumaker, The Hotchkiss School, Lakeville, Connecticut and Jacqueline Dionne Keating, General Brown High School, Dexter, New York.

TEST PREPARATION: The teacher prepares index cards containing a number of situations which arise in a tourist information office. (Examples: a person looking for hotels of a certain price range, maps of subway and bus systems, guided city tours, evening entertainment, etc.)

ADMINISTRATION: The students are tested in groups of two. Each group selects an index card. One student is the worker in the tourist office, and the other is the tourist seeking information. Each conversation should last two to three minutes.

SCORING: Superior creativity and clarity merit the grade "supérieur" ("superior"). Superior creativity or clarity is graded "très bien" ("very good"), and any other honest effort at communication is graded "bien" ("good").

ADDITIONAL SUGGESTIONS: A trial run should be made before the actual test is given. If possible, a large map of the city (e.g., Paris) should be hung in front of the class as reference for the tourist office worker. This test works best after students have studied the city and its various cultural and touristic offerings.

TITLE: On fait des projets (Decisions, Decisions, Decisions . . .)
LEVEL: Intermediate.
SUBMITTED BY: Sally J. Smith, The Academy of the New Church, Girls School, Bryn Athyn, Pennsylvania.
TEST PREPARATION: The teacher prepares a list of topics for a school committee discussion. Each topic is accompanied by specific problems needing resolution and has to do with making plans for a future event.
ADMINISTRATION: The students are tested in groups of four. Each group should contain students of varying degrees of proficiency wherever possible. The teacher chooses a student leader to guide the discussion for each of the groups but the leader is encouraged to enter into the discussion as well. The leader is given the topic and tells the group what they are to plan at this meeting and what questions need to be decided. Discussion should last about ten minutes.
SCORING: Grading can be done on the following scale:
0   no responses
3   comprehensible, but errors in vocabulary or structure
5   comprehensible, with minor errors only
SAMPLE SCRIPT
Le comité chargé par la classe de faire les projets pour un bal. Questions déjà décidées: La date: le 18 décembre. Le lieu: le gymnase. Les invités: tous les élèves de la classe ou de l'école.
QUESTIONS À DÉCIDER
A. Le thème de la décoration   B. Les rafraîchissements
Le comité chargé par le cercle français de faire les projets pour un dîner français.
Questions déjà décidées: la date: dans 3 semaines

QUESTIONS À DÉCIDER
  A. Le lieu
  B. Les invités
  C. La décoration
  D. Le repas
SAMPLE SCRIPT
  Committee I: in charge of planning a school prom.
  Issues already decided: Date—December 18
                             Place—The gymnasium
                             Guests—All students
  Decisions still needed:
    A. A theme for the decorations
    B. Refreshments
  Committee II: in charge of planning a French dinner.
  Issues already decided: Date—3 weeks from today
  Decisions still needed:
    A. Place
    B. Guests
    C. Decorations
    D. Food

TITLE: Comptes-tu aller au concert "rock"? (Are You Going to That Concert?)

LEVEL: Intermediate.
SUBMITTED BY: Barbara B. Dow, Tulsa Junior College, Tulsa, Oklahoma.
TEST PREPARATION: The students draw numbers both for partners and for order of presentation or recording. The primary object is for the partners to be able to get together at the proper time and place. The secondary object is to give the partner a little information about the event. A deck of "events" is prepared.
ADMINISTRATION: The students are paired off and are given a few minutes to review such words as "quand" ("when"), "où" ("where"), "qui" ("who"), etc. They pick a card from the deck which tells them where they are going to meet.
  The students may either perform for the rest of the class, or they may record their conversation on tape.
SCORING: If all the essential information is exchanged and an additional phrase or two (the name of the rock star, etc.) is added, a grade of "très bien" ("very good") is awarded. If either the time or the place is omitted, the grade of "bien" ("good") is awarded. "Convenable" ("satisfactory") is given for any exchange at all which consists of two or three utterances from each participant.

TITLE: Perdu en ville (Finding Your Way in a Big City)
LEVEL: Intermediate.
SUBMITTED BY: Lizbeth Huyer, Hatboro-Horsham High School, Horsham, Pennsylvania.
TEST PREPARATION: The class is divided into two groups. Half of the students are given maps of various cities. A packet of cards containing the names of various places in the cities is prepared.
ADMINISTRATION: The students with the maps are designated "police officers," and the others are "lost tourists." Each tourist must find a policeman to help him find his way. The tourists pick a card from the packet which indicates their destination, and they ask the police officers for instructions on how to get there. They must follow the directions and indicate on an unmarked map the location to which they have been directed.
SCORING: If the tourist arrives at the correct location, the police officer has given good directions and they both pass the test. If not, the tourist must draw another destination and ask another police officer for instructions.

TITLE: En famille (All in the Family)
LEVEL: Intermediate or advanced.
SUBMITTED BY: Martha Brassil, Lincoln Academy, Newcastle, Maine.
TEST PREPARATION: The teacher prepares a list of situations which a family would be likely to discuss and which encompass the interests and abilities of the students.
ADMINISTRATION: The class is divided into groups of four or five, and each group represents a family. One student will play the mother, one the father, and the others will be the children, probably teenagers. The teacher gives each family a situation for discussion. All the groups may have their discussions simultaneously, with the teacher visiting each group, or the groups may perform one at a time to facilitate scoring. The test may be given immediately, or the students may be given five minutes to organize their ideas according to their needs and abilities.
SCORING: Each student is scored on a basis of participation. The test may be scored on a scale of 1 to 3.
  1. minimal participation
  2. active participation
  3. active, enthusiastic participation; leadership role
SAMPLE SCRIPTS
  1. Qu'est-ce qu'on va faire dimanche?
  2. Pourquoi est-ce que les enfants sont rentrés à la maison à minuit et demi hier soir?
  3. Il faut dépenser moins d'argent.
  4. Qui a bosselé l'aile gauche de la voiture?

SAMPLE SCRIPTS
1. What should we do on Sunday?
2. Why did the children come home after midnight last night?
3. We have to cut down on our spending.
4. Who dented the left fender of the car?

TITLE: Comment réagissez-vous? (How Would You React?)
LEVEL: Intermediate or advanced.
SUBMITTED BY: Eleanor Hooker, Cambridge High & Latin, Cambridge, Massachussets.
TEST PREPARATION: Each student thinks of a situation which could possibly raise a moral question. (Example: Vous allez passer un examen. Vous n'avez pas étudié. Allez-vous tricher?)
ADMINISTRATION: One student at a time presents her situation to the class. The other students then react to the situation and to one another's comments.
SCORING: The grades of "très bien" ("very good"), "bien" ("good"), and "parlez davantage" ("speak more") are given based on the fluency of the conversation, the interaction between the students, and the appropriateness of the remarks.
ADDITIONAL SUGGESTIONS: A trial run might be helpful before the test.
TEST PREPARATION: Example: You're going to take a test that you didn't study for. Will you cheat?

TITLE: Bagarre amicale (A Friendly Squabble)
LEVEL: Intermediate or advanced.
SUBMITTED BY: Françoise L. Bonnemoy, American School of Paris, Saint-Cloud, France.
TEST PREPARATION: The students are given a choice of two or three topics of conversation, all concerning an event they both supposedly attended. (Examples: a ski trip, a field trip, a chemistry experiment, etc.) They are given a few minutes to organize their ideas.
ADMINISTRATION: The students are tested in groups of two. The teacher and the students sit in a circle with the two participants seated next to each other. One student starts telling the class about what went on at the event, and the other student teases him about it. After two or three minutes have elapsed, the students change roles.
SCORING: Each time a student succeeds in ribbing the other one, he gets a point, as long as the remarks are related to the topic.
SAMPLE SCRIPT
A: Formidable, le séjour à la montagne! J'ai skié et j'ai passé ma première étoile!
B: Bien sûr, tu plaisais au moniteur!

SAMPLE SCRIPT
  A: That ski trip was really great—I got my first star!
  B: Of course you did—the instructor liked you!

TITLE: La vie (non) scolaire (Nonscholastic Life)
LEVEL: Intermediate or advanced.
SUBMITTED BY: Cathy Linder, The Windsor School, Flushing, New York.
TEST PREPARATION: The teacher prepares index cards containing the name of a family member, and one line explaining the role he must play.
ADMINISTRATION: The students are tested in groups of three. Each student picks a card, telling him the personality he is to portray. At the intermediate level, the situation may be explained in English; at the advanced level, it is told in French. The students are given five minutes to prepare what they want to say. They must talk in front of the class for ten minutes, and the class must be able to summarize and evaluate the performances.
SCORING: At the teacher's discretion, scoring may be left to the class. If they found the sketch convincing and understandable, the students in the group receive an A. If it was convincing but not too understandable or understandable but not too convincing, the group will get a B. If it was neither convincing nor understandable and an honest effort was made, the group will receive a C.
SAMPLE SCRIPT
  You failed your math test, and both your parents have to sign it. The night before the test, you wanted to go out with your friends. Your parents agreed only after you promised them you had finished all your work. In effect, you did no work at all that night.

TITLE: Pour ou contre l'exploration spaciale? (Special Exploration: Pro or Con?)
LEVEL: Advanced.
SUBMITTED BY: Christiane Zue, Windsor High School, Windsor, Vermont.
TEST PREPARATION: A few sentences in French presenting the subject can be read to the students, who should be familiar with some of the vocabulary involved and with the cost of such programs.
ADMINISTRATION: There will be six students on each debating team, three pro and three con. Ten minutes should be sufficient for all the students to express their points of view. Students not participating in the debate will be the judges. After the ten minutes have elapsed, the judges must decide which side gave a more convincing argument.
SCORING: According to the judges' decision, the winners will receive ten points, and the losers will receive seven points.

TITLE: Sauvez-vous de l'enfer! (*Huis Clos*) (**Save Us!** *No Exit*)

LEVEL: Advanced.

SUBMITTED BY: Ann J. Sorrell, South Burlington High School, South Burlington, Vermont.

TEST PREPARATION: After having studied the play *Huis Clos*, a series of index cards is placed in an envelope, each one containing either the name of one of the characters in the play or the author's name. Under each name is a set of instructions telling the character what she must do.

ADMINISTRATION: The class is divided into four groups. Each group chooses a card which tells them who they are and what their task is. One person reads her group's task to the class. After fifteen minutes of preparation time, each group will try to prove that its character has been misplaced. Other people from other groups may interrupt. "Sartre" may interrupt also.

SCORING: Each group should be graded collectively, according to the number of different points brought out and participation of its members.

A   strong points, good participation

B   good participation

C   minimal effort

SAMPLE SCRIPT

Vous êtes Inès!

Vous devriez condamner Garcin et Estelle à l'enfer. Il faut prouver leur culpabilité et votre innocence pour que Sartre vous libère de l'enfer. Soyez sûre d'utiliser toutes les caractéristiques de votre personnalité pour vous aider à le convaincre.

After all three groups have tried to convince Sartre of their character's innocence, Sartre can decide on the basis of who had the best argument whom he will release from eternal damnation.

ADDITIONAL SUGGESTIONS: The teacher can play the role of the author and be the devil's advocate thus forcing the students to defend their character. This idea can also be adapted to almost any story or play.

SAMPLE SCRIPT

You are Ines!

You have to condemn Garcin and Estelle to hell. You must prove their guilt and your innocence so that Sartre will free you from hell. Be sure to use all your personality traits when trying to convince him.

TITLE: "Dean Martin Roast"

LEVEL: Advanced.

SUBMITTED BY: Patricia A. Haupt, Palmyra Area Senior High School, Palmyra, Pennsylvania.

TEST PREPARATION: For each student in the class, a number is written on a slip of paper.

ADMINISTRATION: Each student picks a number. This number tells them his week to be roasted. For example, the student who picked number 3 will be roasted on the third week. The students will all know in advance the "victim" of the next week's roast, and they can prepare their remarks.

The roast consists of a group of individuals, usually a group of close friends, getting together for the purpose of "honoring" another friend. Traits of character are discussed, hidden incidents from the past exposed in an amusing manner, etc. At the end of the roast, the "victim" has the opportunity to retort. As an added incentive, the teacher may wish to sacrifice herself and volunteer to be roasted on the last week.

SCORING: The students receive one point for each remark they make about the "victim." There is a maximum of three points. The "victim" receives one point for each retort he makes. There is a maximum of 10 points.

TITLE: Le naufrage (Shipwrecked!)
LEVEL: Advanced.
SUBMITTED BY: Patricia A. Haupt, Palmyra Area Senior High School, Palmyra, Pennsylvania.
TEST PREPARATION: Review of expressions of emotions.
ADMINISTRATION: The teacher chooses two students. One plays the role of the interviewer, and the other one is the shipwrecked person returned home safely after having been lost at sea for two weeks. After an accident at sea, the student is washed ashore on a deserted island. The interviewer asks the shipwrecked person about her feelings out at sea, the rescue, etc.
SCORING: If the class feels that the interview was convincing and the characters appeared to be sincere, the pair receives the grade "sauvé!" ("You're saved!"). If not, the shipwrecked person is sent back to sea, the interviewer must find another person to interview, and the shipwrecked person must wait to be rescued by another interviewer.

TITLE: Comment vendre un produit? (The Art of Selling a Product)
LEVEL: Advanced.
SUBMITTED BY: Jill McKeever Bowers, Brimmer & May School, Chestnut Hill, Massachusetts.
TEST PREPARATION: The students choose a product currently marketed or make up their own product.
ADMINISTRATION: The students are divided into teams of three. Each group will choose a product or create an imaginary one for which they develop an advertisement for a magazine or a commercial for television. Each member of the trio will have a different role in drawing up the advertisement. The market researcher will consider the public at whom the product is aimed. The artist will prepare the visual presentation. The writer will narrate or make up a wording that corresponds to the idea and the visuals.

SCORING: The students are rated "excellent," "très bien" ("very good"), "bien" ("good") and "moyen" ("fair") according to the following criteria:
1. Were the students organized as a team?
2. Did they successfully communicate their ideas to each other and to the class?
3. Was their interaction free-flowing?
4. How original was the presentation?

TITLE: Les défenses II (Defense—Part II)
LEVEL: Beginner, intermediate, or advanced.
SUBMITTED BY: Anne Grundstrom, University of Wisconsin, Madison, Wisconsin.
TEST PREPARATION: The teacher prepares, or the students submit, a series of "crime cards," each containing an infraction as well as the situational details.
ADMINISTRATION: The students select a partner to form pairs of attorneys and plaintiffs—"le procureur" and "le plaignant." The attorney selects a "crime," revealing to the plaintiff and to the class the nature of the accusation and her desire to either defend or convict the plaintiff. Each student may present his case briefly and must respond to any inquiry posed by the class or the other student.
SCORING: The class and the teacher should give global evaluations of the performance in terms of comprehensibility and appropriateness.
SAMPLE SCRIPT
1. Vous êtes homme d'affaires et vous êtes coupable de discrimmination contre une employée suédoise.
2. Votre société est membre du Syndicat des Camionneurs mais vous refusez de payer le salaire demandé par ce syndicat.
3. Vous êtes sénateur. Vous avez trompé votre femme et volé de l'argent du gouvernement.
SAMPLE SCRIPT
1. You are a businessman, and you discriminated against a Swedish employee.
2. Your trucking society is part of the Transport Workers Union, but you have refused to pay the salary demanded by this union.
3. You are a Senator. You cheated on your wife and stole government funds.

Selected Bibliography

Clark, John L. D. *Foreign Language Testing: Theory & Practice*. Philadelphia: Center for Curriculum Development, 1972.

Jones, Randall L., and Spolsky, Bernard, eds. *Testing Language Proficiency*. Arlington, Va.: Center of Applied Linguistics, 1975.

Jorstad, Helen L. "Testing as Communication," in *The Challenge of Communication*. Edited by Gilbert A. Jarvis. The ACTFL Review of Foreign Language Education, vol. 6. Skokie, Ill.: National Textbook, 1974.

Palmer, Leslie, and Spolsky, Bernard, eds. *Papers on Language Testing: 1967–1974*. Washington, D.C.: Teachers of English to Speakers of Other Languages, 1975.

Schulz, Renate A. and Bartz, Walter H. "Free to Communicate," in *Perspective: A New Freedom*. Edited by Gilbert A. Jarvis. The ACTFL Review of Foreign Language Education, vol. 7. Skokie, Ill.: National Textbook, 1975.

Valette, Rebecca M. *Modern Language Testing*, 2d ed. New York: Harcourt Brace Jovanovich, 1977.

NTC PROFESSIONAL MATERIALS

ACTFL Review

Published annually in conjunction with the American Council on the Teaching of Foreign Languages

NEW PERSPECTIVES, NEW DIRECTIONS IN FOREIGN LANGUAGE EDUCATION, ed.
Birckbichler, Vol. 20 (1990)

MODERN TECHNOLOGY IN FOREIGN LANGUAGE EDUCATION: APPLICATIONS AND
PROJECTS, ed. Smith, Vol. 19 (1989)

MODERN MEDIA IN FOREIGN LANGUAGE EDUCATION: THEORY AND
IMPLEMENTATION, ed. Smith, Vol. 18 (1987)

DEFINING AND DEVELOPING PROFICIENCY: GUIDELINES, IMPLEMENTATIONS, AND
CONCEPTS, ed. Byrnes, Vol. 17 (1986)

FOREIGN LANGUAGE PROFICIENCY IN THE CLASSROOM AND BEYOND, ed. James, Vol. 16 (1984)

TEACHING FOR PROFICIENCY, THE ORGANIZING PRINCIPLE, ed. Higgs, Vol. 15 (1983)

PRACTICAL APPLICATIONS OF RESEARCH IN FOREIGN LANGUAGE TEACHING, ed. James, Vol. 14 (1982)

CURRICULUM, COMPETENCE, AND THE FOREIGN LANGUAGE TEACHER, ed. Higgs, Vol. 13 (1981)

Professional Resources

CENTRAL STATES CONFERENCE TITLES (annuals)

A TESOL PROFESSIONAL ANTHOLOGY: CULTURE

A TESOL PROFESSIONAL ANTHOLOGY: GRAMMAR AND COMPOSITION

A TESOL PROFESSIONAL ANTHOLOGY: LISTENING, SPEAKING, AND READING

THE COMPLETE ESL/EFL RESOURCE BOOK, Scheraga

ABC's OF LANGUAGES AND LINGUISTICS, Hayes, et al.

AWARD-WINNING FOREIGN LANGUAGE PROGRAMS: PRESCRIPTIONS FOR SUCCESS, Sims and Hammond

PUZZLES AND GAMES IN LANGUAGE TEACHING, Danesi

GUIDE TO SUCCESSFUL AFTER-SCHOOL ELEMENTARY FOREIGN LANGUAGE PROGRAMS, Lozano

COMPLETE GUIDE TO EXPLORATORY FOREIGN LANGUAGE PROGRAMS, Kennedy and DeLorenzo

INDIVIDUALIZED FOREIGN LANGUAGE INSTRUCTION, Grittner and LaLeike

LIVING IN LATIN AMERICA: A CASE STUDY IN CROSS-CULTURAL COMMUNICATION, Gorden

ORAL COMMUNICATION TESTING, Linder

ELEMENTARY FOREIGN LANGUAGE PROGRAMS: AN ADMINISTRATOR'S HANDBOOK, Lipton

PRACTICAL HANDBOOK TO ELEMENTARY FOREIGN LANGUAGE PROGRAMS, Second edition, Lipton

SPEAK WITH A PURPOSE! Urzua, et al.

TEACHING LANGUAGES IN COLLEGE, Rivers

TEACHING CULTURE: STRATEGIES FOR INTERCULTURAL COMMUNICATION, Seelye

TEACHING FRENCH: A PRACTICE GUIDE, Rivers

TEACHING GERMAN: A PRACTICAL GUIDE, Rivers, et al.

TEACHING SPANISH: A PRACTICAL GUIDE, Rivers, et al.

TRANSCRIPTION AND TRANSLITERATION, Wellisch

YES! YOU CAN LEARN A FOREIGN LANGUAGE, Goldin, et al.

LANGUAGES AT WORK (VIDEO), Mueller

CULTURAL LITERACY AND INTERACTIVE LANGUAGE INSTRUCTION (VIDEO), Mueller

For further information or a current catalog, write:
National Textbook Company
a division of *NTC Publishing Group*
4255 West Touhy Avenue
Lincolnwood, Illinois 60646-1975 U.S.A.